Dear Fellow Psychology Teachers:

Providing psychology teachers with effective and engaging teaching tips is an important goal of the Psychology Community (formerly the Psychology Special Interest Group). What is the Psychology Community? The Psychology Community is part of the National Council for the Social Studies (NCSS); its members share expertise in and concern for the field of psychology. In conjunction with the NCSS, the Psychology Community strives to help teachers of pre-college and advanced placement psychology courses.

Bob Stahl founded the Psychology Special Interest Group (Psych SIG) in the 1970s after he realized that psychology teachers lacked a network within their schools. Following his tenure, Jim Matiya and Dale Kinney continued the quest to provide these teachers with unique teaching techniques and strategies for the classroom. Starting in 2005, Daria Schaffeld, Lindsay Hackman, and Joe Geiger proudly assumed leadership of this interest group with the hope of continuing to unite psychology teachers across the United States and Canada.

Membership is always open and lasts for three years. With a $30 membership fee, you receive three newsletters a year that include lesson ideas, stories, comics, local and national conventions, and interesting facts—all in the field of psychology. Furthermore, you receive a Psychology Community pencil and T-shirt. Meetings are held annually, usually in late November or early December, at the NCSS Conference to discuss the future of psychology in the classroom and to share best practice ideas with one another.

To join the Psychology Community, a person first needs to become a member of the NCSS. This can be done by going to the NCSS Web site at http://www.socialstudies.org/. Next, contact Lindsay Hackman at lindsay.hackman@d214.org.

For more information about the Psychology Community, please check out our Web site at http://sigs.socialstudies.org/pages/bin/view/Psychology/WebHome?rev=3, or you can access our site through a link on the NCSS home page. You can also contact one of the tri-chair members of the organization with any questions you have about psychology. We are always willing to help you be the best psychology teacher you can be.

Sincerely,

Daria Schaffeld
Prospect High School
801 W. Kensington Road
Mt. Prospect, IL 60056
daria.schaffeld@d214.org

Lindsay Hackman-Cushing
Buffalo Grove High School
1100 W. Dundee Road
Buffalo Grove, IL 60089
lindsay.hackman@d214.org

Joe Geiger
Carl Sandburg High School
13300 S. LaGrange Road
Orland Park, IL 60462
jgeiger@d230.org

Teaching Tips

to accompany

Charles T. Blair-Broeker
and Randal M. Ernst

Thinking About Psychology, 2/e

Worth Publishers

Teaching Tips Booklet
to accompany Charles T. Blair-Broeker and Randal M. Ernst's *Thinking About Psychology*, 2/e

ISBN 1-4292-0959-3

Worth Publishers
41 Madison Avenue
New York, NY 10010

www.worthpublishers.com

Table of Contents for
Thinking About Psychology, 2/e

Charles T. Blair-Broeker and Randal M. Ernst

➤ **Therapy Chapter**

- Module 32: Psychological Therapies
- Module 33: Biomedical Therapies

➤ **Social Psychology Chapter**

- Module 34: Social Thinking and Social Influence

- Module 35: Social Relations

- Module 36: Cross-Cultural Psychology

Additional Activities:

Teaching Tips

Activity 1: Psychology's Family Tree

Contributed by Whitney Blankenship
Leander High School
Leander, Texas

Ms. Blankenship is currently in her 13th year with the Leander Independent School District in Leander, Texas. Over the years, she has taught World Geography, U.S. History, International Baccalaureate History of the Americas, and International Baccalaureate Psychology, as well as AP U.S. History and Pre-AP World Geography. In May 2005, she was named a regional finalist for H-E-B's Excellence in Education Award. She is working on her doctorate in social studies education at The University of Texas at Austin.

I developed this activity after noting that my students often have a hard time connecting the social, historical, and cultural events that shaped the development of psychology. Students tend to easily remember the more sensational bits and pieces—such as the idea that mental disorders are evidence of demonic possession—but they have a harder time connecting major ideas such as Darwin's development of evolutionary theory, or the cultural climate of the Victorian era, with Freud's theories. I have tried timeline activities in the past, but I found that they were too linear and that students did not grasp how all of these events were interconnected.

This activity is used as a review at the end of the History and Perspectives unit. Students are divided into teams to complete the project and are given roughly one and a half periods to complete the project. The last part of the second class period is used for presentations.

After completing the project and viewing the representations of the other groups, students tend to have a better understanding of the connections between what has gone on outside of psychology and the development of psychology as a science over time.

Psychology's Family Tree

To complete this project, the class will be divided into two large teams. Each team will be responsible for determining how they will represent the family tree and dividing up the task to complete the project. Each person on the team must contribute to the final effort. This task will serve as a review of the material we have been covering for the past three weeks, in addition to the review guide you will receive today. You will have the remainder of the period today and one hour of the next period to complete the project.

The goal: Create a family tree for the discipline of psychology. The tree should include elements from the history of psychology, your timelines, each of the major perspectives, and the subfields. You should use your notes and textbook to locate information.

How your team chooses to represent the family tree is up to you. It can be a genealogical chart, an actual tree, or some other representation. The key is to show where psychology as a science came from and how it has developed over time. In addition, it should also show how the various perspectives and subfields, events, and people are connected. It should be fairly detailed, but remember that you only have two periods to work on it, so plan accordingly.

Each group will display its family tree during the last 30 minutes of the next class so that everyone can see how it was put together. You should plan on being able to show (briefly) the connections from beginnings to the present.

It is guaranteed that you will have a question about psychology's development on the exam. It is to your benefit to make sure that you understand everything that is on your team's tree and how those connections work. If you don't understand, ask your team members!

Your grade for the project will be based on the following:

1. How well the group worked toward the goal (I'll be watching!)
2. Creativity (how creative the representation is, as well as any other creative elements included, such as pictures, 3-D modeling, life-size depictions, etc.)
3. Whether the connections make sense in relation to how psychology developed over time (i.e., you don't have pre-scientific psychology events occurring after scientific psychology events)
4. Whether you use a substantial number of key events, people, and experiments to illustrate the ties between the various perspectives and subfields (however, they should *not* be the main focus)
5. How clearly you delineated between pre-scientific and scientific psychology
6. How clearly you showed the connections between the various perspectives and their roots

Each item will be graded on a scale of 1 to 10 (10 being excellent), for a total of 60 points.

Activity 2: Dinner Party with Dead Psychologists

Contributed by Laura Brandt and Stephanie Neuberger

Adlai E. Stevenson High School
Chicago, Illinois

Ms. Brandt currently teaches AP Psychology and AP U.S. History at Adlai E. Stevenson High School in the northwest suburbs of Chicago, Illinois. She received her bachelor's degree in social studies secondary education from the University of Illinois, Urbana–Champaign. She received her master's degree in American history from Northern Illinois University and a second master's degree in psychology at DePaul University. She also studied at Oxford University in London while working on her master's degree in history. In addition, Ms. Brandt is a reader for the AP psychology exam and a consultant for the College Board for teachers beginning AP psychology courses. She also currently serves as the chair for Teachers of Psychology in Secondary Schools, which represents high school teachers in the American Psychological Association. She also sponsors the Psychology Club at Stevenson High School and coached girls' track and field for nine years.

Ms. Neuberger currently teaches AP Psychology at Adlai E. Stevenson High School. She received her bachelor's degree from Indiana University, a master's degree in education from National Louis University, and a second master's degree in educational leadership from Northern Illinois University. She studied in Spain during her undergraduate studies and is currently the team leader for the AP Psychology team at Stevenson High School. Ms. Neuberger has served as a reader for the AP psychology exam and on the board for the Sociology Teachers of Illinois.

This activity is best used in the History unit. The activity is intended to introduce students to the numerous psychologists they will learn about over the course of the academic year. The activity is intended to last for two 50-minute periods over two days but may be modified to fit different scheduling formats.

Dinner Party With Dead Psychologists

Sources for many of these include:
http://elvers.udayton.edu/history/welcome.htm
http://psychclassics.yorku.ca/
http://www.dialogical.net/psychology/noteables.html
http://psych.athabascau.ca/html/aupr/history.shtml

Psychologists:

Alfred Adler (1870–1937)
John B. Watson (1878–1958)
Sir Francis Galton (1822–1911)
Karen Horney (1885–1952)
Jean Piaget (1896–1980)
Anna Freud (1895–1982)
Abraham Maslow (1908–1970)
Wilhelm Wundt (1832–1920)
Carl Jung (1875–1961)
Hermann Ebbinghaus (1850–1909)
William James (1842–1910)
G. Stanley Hall (1844–1924)
Edward Thorndike (1874–1949)
Ivan Pavlov (1849–1936)
B. F. Skinner (1904–1990)
Erik Erikson (1902–1994)
Carl Rogers (1902–1987)
Charles Darwin (1809–1882)
Sigmund Freud (1856–1939)
E. B. Titchener (1867–1927)
Mary Whiton Calkins (1863–1930)
Margaret Floy Washburn (1871–1930)

Gordon Allport (1897–1967)
John Dewey (1859–1952)
Gustav Fechner (1801–1887)
Max Wertheimer (1880–1943)
Roger Sperry (1913–1994)

Kenneth Clark (1914–2005)
Edward Tolman (1886–1959)
Lawrence Kohlberg (1927–1987)
Alfred Binet (1857–1911)

Project:

This is an individual project in which you will need to impersonate a famous dead (or nearly dead) psychologist. You may select a psychologist from the attached list or create a proposal for an alternate psychologist. Choices will be given on a first-come first-serve basis.

1. Create a poster that represents your psychologist. The poster should include—but is not limited to—the following criteria:
    a. Picture (3 points)
    b. Birth/death dates (1 point)
    c. Contribution to the field of psychology/historical impact (5 points)
    d. An interesting fact that most would not know (1 point)
    e. How this individual's research is important to modern-day psychology; if this person were alive today, how he/she might apply his/her theory or research (5 points)
2. Develop a question from your psychologist's perspective for each of the other dead psychologists. The questions should be content driven and demonstrate that you have some basic knowledge of what type of research that individual conducted. (25 points) (I will also need a copy of your questions.)
3. Create a costume for your psychologist. His/her costume may be either literal or metaphorical. (10 points)
4. Complete a brief resume for this individual. The resume should include educational background, experience, publications, and extracurricular activities or organizations. (20 points) (This will be turned in as well as the questions for the other psychologists.)

Presentation:

Day 1: Each psychologist will present his/her costume and poster during the first day of presentations. They will explain the basic components of their theory and how it relates to modern research.

Day 2: The dead psychologists will mingle as if at a dinner party and ask each other the questions that they have created. (If you would like to bring something to eat to share with the class, feel free; it would be fun if you can connect the food to your psychologist somehow.)

Table Assignments for Dead Psychologists:

Table 1
Alfred Adler
John Watson
Sir Francis Galton
G. Stanley Hall
Edward Tolman

Table 3
Gustav Fechner
Anna Freud
Abraham Maslow
Wilhelm Wundt
B. F. Skinner

Table 5
Carl Jung
William James
Mary Whiton Calkins
Roger Sperry
Alfred Binet

Table 2
Gordon Allport
Karen Horney
Jean Piaget
Hermann Ebbinghaus
Charles Darwin

Table 4
Edward Thorndike
Erik Erikson
Carl Rogers
Margaret Floy Washburn
Kenneth Clark

Table 6
Sigmund Freud
E. B. Titchener
John Dewey
Max Wertheimer
Lawrence Kohlberg

Follow-Up:

Based on the questions that each of the psychologists has created for one another, we will have an open-note quiz (using any notes you took during the dinner party) to evaluate your knowledge of each of the psychologists. (25–30 points)

Amended from L. Browning at DePaul University, 2004.

Activity 3: The Outrageous Celebrity

Contributed by Kelly A. Cavanaugh
Career Center
Winston-Salem, North Carolina

Ms. Cavanaugh has been teaching AP Psychology since 2002 and has been the online course instructor/developer since 2004. She received her bachelor's degree in psychology from Dartmouth College and her master's degree in liberal studies from the University of North Carolina at Greensboro.

"The Outrageous Celebrity" is designed to help students understand the major psychological perspectives. This activity also gives students memorable examples of each perspective.

I normally conduct this activity as a partner exercise. The students come up with great examples when they work in pairs and are better equipped to explain their examples to each other.

The day before the activity, I provide students with an outline of the major psychological perspectives. I also direct them to a handy chart in their textbook.

The Outrageous Celebrity

The students are to choose the most outrageous celebrity they can think of, past or present. They should provide a short list of some of the outrageous behaviors this person has exhibited. Then, the students should attempt to explain these behaviors from the point of view of each major psychology perspective. The student's reasoning can be as ridiculous as the behavior itself, as long as it falls in line with the perspective. They don't have to be true! I use Dennis Rodman as my example.

Example:

Dennis Rodman is well known for his outrageous behavior, cross-dressing, and rapidly changing hair color.

Neuroscience:

Perhaps Dennis Rodman has a high level of estrogen that makes him feel as though he should wear women's clothes.

Evolutionary:

Dennis Rodman's tall height and athleticism are traits that are naturally selected for; however, his cross-dressing tendencies are counterintuitive to him passing on his own genes. His ancestors were most likely tall and athletic as well.

Behavior Genetics:

We should examine Dennis's genetic background to see whether his behaviors come from his family or are a product of his NBA environment.

Psychodynamic:

Dennis was traumatized as a child when he was not permitted to have a Halloween costume. He has repressed the memory but, as a result, dresses in outrageous clothing to try and overcompensate for his loss as a child.

Behavioral:

Dennis Rodman's father and grandfather both were cross-dressers and frequently dyed their hair. Dennis observed this throughout his life and is now imitating the same behavior.

Cognitive:

Dennis Rodman interprets his role in the NBA as needing to create attention for his team. As a result, he thinks that by cross-dressing, dying his hair, and tattooing his body, his team will get the positive attention it requires.

Social-Cultural:

Perhaps in the NBA culture, these behaviors occur often and are widely accepted; thus, Dennis Rodman believes his behavior to be typical and not out of the ordinary.

Activity 4: Counting Shoes

Contributed by Randy Ernst
Lincoln Public Schools
Lincoln, Nebraska

Mr. Ernst taught psychology at Lincoln High School, North Star High Schools, and Nebraska Wesleyan University. He is a co-author of the *National Standards for the Teaching of High School Psychology*, co-editor of the American Psychological Association's *Activities Handbook for the Teaching of Psychology (Vol. IV)*, and author of the College Board's *Teacher's Guide for Advanced Placement Psychology*. Randy has chaired the Teachers of Psychology in Secondary Schools (TOPSS) executive board, served on the College Board's AP Psychology Test Development Committee, and has been a table leader, question leader, and exam leader at the annual Advanced Placement Psychology Reading. He has authored or co-authored several TOPSS unit plans and has worked to infuse positive psychology across the K–12 curriculum. Mr. Ernst has provided in-service on the teaching of psychology to teachers around the United States and Canada and is an international psychology consultant for the College Board. Honors include Nebraska's 2006 Social Studies Educator of the Year Award, the National Association for the Advancement of Colored People's (Nebraska Chapter) 2004 Service to Children Award, and Time Warner's "Crystal Apple" National Teacher Award. Both the American Psychological Association and the University of Nebraska have recognized Mr. Ernst for excellence in teaching.

The number of shoes women own compared to men can be used to demonstrate several statistical and methodological issues. Students survey friends or acquaintances to collect data on the number of shoes they own. I've done this activity dozens of times, and it has always generated a statistically significant effect with a sample size as small as 20 (10 females, 10 males).

Counting Shoes

Procedure:

Tell each student to gather data from 10 females and 10 males, recording the number of shoes owned by each. Specifically, they should ask, "How many pairs of shoes do you own?" They should try not to stray from the target question if data are gathered orally.

Have students graph the data set (frequency histograms, box-plots), calculate measures of central tendency, and test for differences between means using a t-test.

Discussion:

This activity comes from Steven Sterns, who found that in one class, females had 16.2 pairs on average, while males had 6.42 pairs (t [98] = 7.80, $p < .001$, $r = .62$). Sterns states that samples sizes of 20 participants routinely produce a large and statistically significant ($p < .05$) gender effect on the number of shoes owned.

Several statistical and methodological issues should be discussed following this activity. They include:

A. Outliers. Unlike other data sets collected in class (such as height), these data are likely to generate outliers. The use of box-plots will show the outliers readily. Have students calculate summary statistics and t-test results on data sets with and without the outliers. Discuss the practice of removing outliers from data sets.

B. Effect of sample size on statistical power. Aggregating class data will show how larger sample size leads to more statistical power and a smaller p-value.

C. Operationalizing variables. What constitutes a shoe? Are boots included? Flip-flops? Do shoes owned but no longer worn count? Teachers facilitate appreciation of this issue by having students work together to shape the wording of the research question.

D. Self-report validity. The thread can lead to discussions on exaggeration, social expectation or desirability, and selective memory. How might the data have differed if people had counted their shoes instead of estimating the number?

E. Students find this activity amusing, but it can also provide for a serious discussion of what appears to be a trivial gender difference. Much of what has been found to differ between sexes has been pinned on biological differences. Have students hypothesize reasons as to why women tend to own more shoes (norms, personality) and suggest ways to test their hypotheses.

F. Cultural differences. Would this gender difference exist in all segments of our country? Would it be found in other countries?

Special note: Calculating t-tests is relatively simple using an Excel spreadsheet. Follow the instructions found in an Excel user's guide or on Web sites addressing this procedure.

Activity 5: The Neuron Dance

Contributed by Mary Ann Graham
Bassett High School
Bassett, Virginia

Ms. Graham has been teaching for the past 10 years. She teaches General Psychology and AP Psychology. Teaching is her passion, and she wants to spread that fire to her students. Her goal is to inspire young minds to learn as much as possible. When Ms. Graham is not teaching, she loves to spend time with her husband, Bradley, and her son, Joshua. She also enjoys traveling, taking photographs, and scrapbooking.

Teaching about the neuron used to be difficult. I had a hard time getting students to remember the order and names of the parts of a neuron. Making the process memorable is the key to remembering. I use what I call the "neuron dance" to help visual and kinesthetic learners.

The Neuron Dance

For this activity, we will use different body parts to represent each part of the neuron. Our left hand is the dendrite. Hold your left hand so that your fingers are spread and your arm is very close to your body. This represents the "bushy branches" of the dendrite and the fact that it is shorter than the axon. Next, use your body as the cell body. Your right arm is the axon. Hold your right arm straight out to your side. This is representing the fact that the axon is the longest part of the neuron. At the end of your right arm is your hand, which represents the terminal branches. The tips of your fingers are representing the terminal buttons.

Now that you have the correct corresponding body parts, you are ready to dance! I demonstrate by passing an imaginary signal through my body. I use a little wiggle to indicate movement. Starting with my dendrites, I move the "impulse" to the cell body, down the axon, to the terminal branches and buttons. Saying the neuron part out loud as the action potential is moving through the neuron helps, too. Yes, you may look a bit foolish, but it works!

Note to Teachers:

Once the students have a good grasp of the neuron parts, I have them stand in a circle. We then practice sending the dance around the room. I have a beginning, which represents the brain, and I have an end, which represents a muscle movement. Using the wave effect, we send a message from the brain for the muscle to move.

Also in class, I will say, "Show me your axon (or other parts of the neuron)," and the students will wave the correct part at me. This gives me an idea of who is still struggling with the concept. You can also use the dance "stance" to demonstrate other things, such as the myelin sheath or conversion from electricity to chemicals.

This activity is neat because when we take our test, I will see many students "doing the dance" in their seats to answer the questions. The kids love this activity and remember it!

Activity 6: Neurotransmitter Skits

Contributed by Jeanne Turner
Linn-Mar High School
Marion, Iowa

Ms. Turner has been teaching for 15 years at a large, suburban high school in the block format. She currently teaches Psychology I, Psychology II, and AP Psychology.

The purpose of this activity is for students to apply their knowledge of neurotransmitters. They will have to think about the actions and ask clarifying questions so that their skit is correct. They will have about 30 minutes in class to outline a script. Each skit should be 2–5 minutes.

Neurotransmitter Skits

Materials Needed:

Puppets with name tags (I make sack puppets, but anything could be used). Name tags are a must so that the audience can check the accuracy of each character's actions.

Directions:

Use the characters listed below to create skits that show what each type of neurotransmitter does. It would be a good idea to check other sources besides your textbook to make sure you truly understand the function of each neurotransmitter.

Cast:

Alice Choline   Donna Dopamine
Sara Tonin   Nora Pinephrine
Gabby Gaba   Enrique Endorphins
Gary Glutamate

1. Design a scenario and write a script that would involve the interaction of at least four of the cast members.
2. Define the "personality" for each of the four characters in the cast. The "personality" should reflect the function of that particular neurotransmitter (example: Gabby and Gary argue about how fast to drive a car).
3. Feel free to add additional characters (the brain, Prozac, etc.) if it helps your story line.

These skits are fairly short but are a creative way to remember what the "characters" do in the brain.

Activity 7: Parts of the Brain

Contributed by Steven Cairns
Ionia High School
Ionia, Michigan

Mr. Cairns is a 14-year teaching veteran, having taught at Roma High School in the Rio Grande Valley of Texas for five years and at Ionia High School for the past nine years in Ionia, Michigan. His undergraduate degree is in history and social science from Kalamazoo College, and he has a master's degree in education and history from Grand Valley State University. He also teaches AP U.S. History and World History. His travels have taken him to all lower 48 states and 30 countries, highlighted by a six-month study abroad experience in Strasbourg, France. In his spare time, Mr. Cairns likes to read, travel, take long walks in the country, and enjoy his two children.

Most students struggle with remembering the functions and locations of key parts of the brain. In the initial lesson for this, students use their textbooks to take notes on each part of the brain, and then they must make a mnemonic device to help them remember the parts. They often work in pairs because this second part can be tricky.

An example:

1. Medulla

    a. In charge of keeping us alive by regulating heartbeat, breathing, etc.

    b. "Seeing *Medusa* would turn you to stone and cause your *medulla* to stop functioning so your vital signs would cease."

2. Reticular Activating System

    a. Screens information and communicates it to appropriate higher parts of the brain, allowing us to be conscious

    b. "The *RAS* causes us to '*rise and shine*' so we can be alert and ready for action."

After they've had this graded and returned to them, we have a brief whole-class discussion in which we exchange mnemonics in order to improve our understanding. The next phase is to have short (10–15 seconds) skits or dialogues during which the other students have to guess what brain part is being portrayed. This can be used as a formative assessment, or the answers can be recorded for a grade.

An example might be:

High School Student 1 (*shouting*): "Your mother wears combat boots, and you are a poopy face!"

High School Student 2: "Oh my gosh, you scared me! That might have hurt my feelings when I was a kid. But as a young adult with more knowledge of the world, I know that your words can't hurt me. In fact, you are the one who looks bad."

(This represents the role of the amygdala, which helps us gauge the emotional impact of situations.)

Finally, they use their notes and knowledge to answer these application questions on a worksheet.

Parts of the Brain

Use your outline about the parts of the brain and carefully match them to the descriptions given below. You may want to briefly add why you put what you did so that if my key differs from your answer but you show logic, you can still get the point. This, however, is optional.

1. Epileptic seizures have become so severe that the two hemispheres of the brain are disconnected during surgery. This quiets the electrical storm raging between the two sides.

2. A blow to the base of the head makes the person wobble and struggle to run.

3. Damage to this area from a stroke makes a person incapable of sewing or doing other things with the sensitive finger nerves because what their fingers are doing can't be interpreted.

4. Damage to this area causes a person not to form memories properly, like the guy in the movie *Memento*.

5. Pressure from a tumor on this part of the brain causes a person to fly off the handle when simple emotional pressures arise. Teens tend to use this part more than their rational frontal lobes when judging situations, causing them to overreact sometimes.

6. A football player hits the back of his helmet on the ground and experiences blurred vision.

7. A malfunction in this organ was once thought to cause synesthesia, a disorder in which letters have colors and sounds make you itch. Certain foods or flavors may have a "pointy" feeling as well.

8. Low brain chemicals and an underdevelopment in this area cause a person to be a hermit who can't play the social game. They just seem odd to other people.

9. Stimulation of this area causes our increased sexual interests as we get older. Understimulation can cause anorexia because normal activity here stimulates girls to eat more so their bodies are ready for childbearing. (Extra credit: starving oneself may make it harder to make a neurotransmitter that in high levels makes a person anxious; which one is it?)

10. A brain injury makes someone sluggish because areas of the brain pertinent to concentration and paying attention aren't notified. (The key here is that higher portions of the brain that need to be stimulated aren't getting notified by this part of the brain. It's more general—not specific just to sensory information.)

11. Crushing of this area causes all vital functions to cease, as when Dale Earnhardt crashed his car into the wall at Daytona.

12. Some cases of dyslexia may be a problem of lack of communication between these *two* regions of the brain. They deal with language comprehension and sight. (Put one *area* and one of the lobes!)

13. Dreams may be the result of your cerebrum trying to make sense of all sorts of signals that this part of the brain sends during sleep.

14. Imprints on the inside of skulls belonging to the supposed human ancestor *Homo habilis* indicate that it was probably during this stage of evolution that speech evolved. It's found on the left hemisphere of the brain, in the front.

Answers: 1. corpus callosum; 2. cerebellum; 3. parietal lobe; 4. hippocampus; 5. amygdala; 6. occipital lobe; 7. thalamus; 8. frontal lobe; 9. hypothalamus (extra credit: serotonin); 10. reticular activating system; 11. medulla; 12. Wernicke's area (in the temporal lobe) and occipital lobe; 13. pons; 14. Broca's area

Activity 8: Making a Brain Mobile

Contributed by Margaret Davidson
L.V. Berkner High School
Richardson, Texas

Ms. Davidson teaches Introductory Psychology, AP Psychology, and Economics at L.V. Berkner High School in Richardson, Texas, where she has taught for 24 years. She was a participant and three-time presenter in the NSF Summer Institute for the Teaching of Psychology at Texas A&M University, served as lead teacher at the Arthur Vining Davis Foundation Psychology Teacher Institute at Nebraska Wesleyan University, and has presented numerous week-long College Board AP Psychology institutes. Ms. Davidson served as chair of Teachers of Psychology in Secondary Schools. She is a recipient of the Richardson Independent School District's RISE Award, *Who's Who Among America's Teachers*, and the Moffet Memorial High School Award from the American Psychological Association's Society of the Teaching of Psychology. She also received the College Board's Southwest Region Special Recognition Award in 2005.

In order to appeal to the varied types of learners in my class, I have students develop a model of the brain to assist in learning the organization, functions, and locations of structures of the brain. The assignment provides a different learning opportunity for tactile and visual learners. The addition of the model key gives students a quick reference sheet for brain structure and function as they review for content assessments. Students have the opportunity to use their creative abilities as they learn the many details necessary for understanding the science of the brain.

Making a Brain Mobile

Your assignment is to create a three-dimensional mobile of the human brain. Your mobile should be approximately the size of a human brain. You should create this mobile out of any material you choose with the exception of perishable food. The goal of this assignment is to develop a model that identifies specific structures of the human brain. Be sure to include a key to identify specific structures and their functions in human behavior, as well as a small graphic representation to exemplify functions.

Directions:

Begin by making a template of the human head by tracing or sketching a human form. Determine the materials that will be used to represent the structures of the brain. Recall that a mobile should be sturdy enough to be used as a study guide and light enough to hang from the ceiling. Research the specific structures of the brain to be represented as to their size, shape, location, and function. See the following listing for minimum requirements. As you begin making your mobile, use as much detail as possible to accurately represent the human brain. Label specific brain structures directly on your mobile.

A written key should be developed that identifies structures of your model and their function; a picture should be included to help you recall the job of that structure. Example: temporal lobe—includes auditory areas that receive auditory information primarily from the opposite ear

Your mobiles will be displayed by hanging from the ceiling of the classroom. In your final presentation, be sure to include a means for hanging your mobile.

Listing of minimum requirements of brain structures to be represented:

Lower brain	Cerebral cortex
Thalamus	Frontal lobe
Hypothalamus	Temporal lobe
Amygdala	Occipital lobe
Cerebellum	Parietal lobe
Reticular formation	Motor cortex
Medulla	Somatosensory cortex
Spinal cord	Auditory cortex
Hippocampus	Visual cortex
Pituitary gland	Broca's area
Corpus callosum	Wernicke's area
Angular gyrus	

Activity 9: Brain Review Project

Contributed by Tammy Dorgan
Larry A. Ryle High School
Union, Kentucky

Ms. Dorgan graduated from Northern Kentucky University in 2003 with a bachelor of arts degree in history and social studies. She has been teaching General Psychology and AP Psychology for three years at Ryle High School in Union, Kentucky. She is currently working on her master's degree in school counseling through Northern Kentucky University. She is a member of the American Psychological Association, Teachers of Psychology in Secondary Schools, National Council for the Social Studies, and Phi Alpha Theta. Ms. Dorgan was named to *Who's Who Among American High School Teachers* in 2006.

This is a project that I use with my students in psychology to review the brain. The benefit of this activity is that it addresses many of the multiple intelligences. The students are very clever, and they seem more interested in the presentations if I give them many options.

Brain Review Project

You may work in groups of three or individually. Please choose one activity from the following selection:

- Write and perform a song about the parts and areas of the brain and their functions. Submit a hard copy of the song. If this is a group presentation, one person should be the writer, one the singer, and one should play an instrument. (individual or group)

- Create a skit about the parts and areas of the brain and their functions. Submit a hard copy of the skit. (group)

- Write and present a poem about the parts and areas of the brain and their functions. (individual)

- Create a PowerPoint presentation with music and clip art. Present it to the class. Submit a copy of the presentation in handout format. (individual or group)

- Create a 3-D model of the brain with the required parts and areas labeled; explain the function of each part. (individual)

- Paint the brain on canvas, depicting the parts and areas listed below; explain the functions to the class. (individual)

- Create a newsletter about the parts and areas of the brain and their functions. Include clip art, borders, and headings. Present your newsletter to the class. (individual)

- Create a poster about the parts and areas of the brain including pictures and functions. Present your poster to the class. The poster must be neat and have a heading, and photos/pictures must be labeled, including the functions. (individual)

Parts and Areas of the Brain:

Amygdala
Angular gyrus
Association areas
Brainstem
Broca's area
Cerebellum
Cerebral cortex
Corpus callosum
Frontal lobe
Hippocampus
Hypothalamus
Medulla
Motor cortex
Occipital lobe
Parietal lobe
Pituitary gland
Reticular formation
Sensory cortex
Temporal lobe
Thalamus
Visual cortex
Wernicke's area

Activity 10: Brain Skits

Contributed by Melanie Montagnon
Mark T. Sheehan High School
Wallingford, Connecticut

Ms. Montagnon is in her seventh year of teaching Social Studies at Mark T. Sheehan High School. She has taught Psychology for the past six years and AP Psychology for the past three years. She graduated from Salve Regina University in 1999 with a bachelor of arts and sciences in secondary education and history. She is currently pursuing a master's degree in psychology.

I have found that most students do not realize that studying the brain is part of a social science course. So, many students are quite shocked when they learn that they must know parts of the brain and their functions. In order to assist in their learning, I have found a few activities and assignments that help the process along.

Brain Skits

Objective:

Create a skit demonstrating how the brain communicates and operates during an everyday situation.

Guidelines:

1. Select a few of your classmates to collaborate with.
2. Decide on a simple situation to role play.
3. Create a skit, including dialogue. Depending on the size of the group, members may have to play more than one role to correctly demonstrate brain functioning.
4. Generate any props needed (i.e., name tags).
5. Practice skit.
6. Act out skit for class.
7. Hand in script.

Answers to Your Questions:

- The skit does not have to be long; it could last 30 seconds to 5 minutes or even longer.
- You should try to incorporate as many brain structures as possible.
- Yes, I am collecting a written skit from each group. The script must be written to demonstrate understanding of how the brain functions.
- Yes, I am grading the acting during the skit.

Grading:

- The written portion has a value of 50 points, collectively.
- The acting has a value of 25 points, individually.

Activity 11: Creating a Two-Dimensional Brain Mobile

Contributed by Melanie Montagnon
Mark T. Sheehan High School
Wallingford, Connecticut

Ms. Montagnon is in her seventh year of teaching Social Studies at Mark T. Sheehan High School. She has taught Psychology for the past six years and AP Psychology for the past three years. She graduated from Salve Regina University in 1999 with a bachelor of arts and sciences in secondary education and history. She is currently pursuing a master's degree in psychology.

I have found that most students do not realize that studying the brain is part of a social science course. So, many students are quite shocked when they learn that they must know parts of the brain and their functions. In order to assist in their learning, I have found a few activities and assignments that help the process along.

Creating a Two-Dimensional Brain Mobile

The Brain unit can be difficult due to the amount of memorization required. To make this task a little easier, you are going to be creating a "brain mobile." This will become your "cheat sheet" when we discuss the parts and functions of the brain.

Steps:

A. Pair up with a classmate and trace your partner's head onto a piece of paper.

B. Draw a brain on both sides of the "head." One side should represent the cerebral cortex, and the other side should represent the lower brain. Make sure that the drawings are accurate in terms of placement!

C. Clearly label all parts of the brain, including:

   1. Cerebral Cortex

     a. Corpus Callosum

     b. Fissure

     c. Frontal Lobe

       – Motor Cortex

       – Prefrontal Area

       – Frontal Association Area

     d. Parietal Lobe

       – Sensory Cortex

     e. Occipital Lobe

       – Primary Visual Cortex

     f. Temporal Lobe

       – Auditory Cortex

   2. Lower Brain

     g. The Limbic System

       – Hypothalamus

       – Amygdala

       – Hippocampus

     h. Thalamus

     i. Cerebellum

     j. Reticular Activating System (RAS)

     k. Pituitary Gland

   3. Hemispheres

   4. Brainstem

D. Draw a visual cue that shows the function of each part.

E. You will be graded on both the correctness and creativeness of your brain mobile. The point value for this assignment is 150 points.

Activity 12: Sensation Lab

Contributed by Laura Brandt and Stephanie Neuberger
Adlai E. Stevenson High School
Chicago, Illinois

This activity is intended to introduce students to working with different concepts in the Sensation and Perception unit. This activity can also be used as a review activity for the unit once students are familiar with the concepts in the unit. This activity can be used as an in-class assignment or as a take-home assignment. It covers some of the basic biological components of the chapter as well as visual illusions and concepts involved with other senses, such as taste.

Ms. Brandt currently teaches AP Psychology and AP U.S. History at Adlai E. Stevenson High School in the northwest suburbs of Chicago, Illinois. She received her bachelor's degree in social studies secondary education from the University of Illinois, Urbana–Champaign. She received her master's degree in American history from Northern Illinois University and a second master's degree in psychology at DePaul University. She also studied at Oxford University in London while working on her master's degree in history. In addition, Ms. Brandt is a reader for the AP psychology exam and a consultant for the College Board for teachers beginning AP psychology courses. She also currently serves as the chair for Teachers of Psychology in Secondary Schools, which represents high school teachers in the American Psychological Association. She also sponsors the Psychology Club at Stevenson High School and coached girls' track and field for nine years.

Ms. Neuberger currently teaches AP Psychology at Adlai E. Stevenson High School. She received her bachelor's degree from Indiana University, a master's degree in education from National Louis University, and a second master's degree in educational leadership from Northern Illinois University. She studied in Spain during her undergraduate studies and is currently the team leader for the AP Psychology team at Stevenson High School. Ms. Neuberger has served as a reader for the AP psychology exam and on the board for the Sociology Teachers of Illinois.

Sensation Lab

Go to the following Web site:
http://www.bbc.co.uk/science/humanbody/body/interactives/senseschallenge/senses.swf

When asked if you have sound on your computer, click on "No."

1. After doing challenge #1, click on the explanation. Why do optical illusions occur?
2. For challenge #3, explain what is happening in this illusion.
3. Explain shadow compensation (from challenge #5).
4. Explain what happens in challenge #6.
5. How does our past experience impact how we process information? (challenge #7)
6. Why do many people have difficulty finding the change in the image in question #9?
7. Why do chili peppers taste hot? (challenge #12)
8. Why are supertasters more sensitive to taste than others? (challenge #13)
9. How is the intensity of sound measured? What impacts the loudness we perceive? (challenge #15)
10. Why are smells often linked to memories? (challenge #20)

Now that you have completed the sense challenge, let's go to the Exploratorium! Go to the following Web site to begin: http://www.exploratorium.edu/exhibits/f_exhibits.html

11. Click on the "Bird in a Cage" illusion. After trying out the illusion, explain what an afterimage is.
12. Click on "Mix-n-Match." Explain why you can create so many different colors out of just three.
13. Choose one other perceptual illusion to look at. Describe it and explain why it works.

Go to the following Web site: http://www.stlukeseye.com/anatomy.asp

14. Why is the eye compared to a camera?
15. What does the cornea do?
16. What does the optic nerve do?
17. What does the pupil do?

Go to the following Web site: http://library.thinkquest.org/J002330

18–20. Click on three different vision ailments and explain them.

Activity 13: The Touch Box

Contributed by Pamela Bowman
Woodrow Wilson High School
Camden, New Jersey

Ms. Bowman is a teacher of social studies and department chairperson at Woodrow Wilson High School in Camden, New Jersey. This year, as her school transitions into small learning communities, she is also the lead teacher for the Social and Human Services community. This is her 34th year at Woodrow Wilson. Since being a reviewer for the first edition of *Thinking About Psychology*, Ms. Bowman has used this text in her behavioral studies classes. She lives in Edgewater Park, New Jersey, and she is married with two grown children who are also in the education field.

Students often think that the sense of touch is not important or that they can always identify items. What they don't think about is how they are still using their other senses to do this. In isolating the sense of touch, suddenly this assignment is not so easy. The students are instructed to look around the house for small, non-valuable items that might be difficult to identify by touch alone. Once in class, the students have a hands-on experience in sensory isolation. It can be like a mini fun house, not too scary if you know what is inside.

The Touch Box

Assignment Guidelines:

1. Secure a box measuring at least 12 inches wide, 12 inches long, and 12 inches high. A shoebox is too small.

2. Collect 10 to 15 small items that you feel will be difficult to identify by touch alone (for example: feather, cotton ball). Do not put anything in the box that might harm or discolor anyone. No live or dead animals. No food items. Do not use anything valuable.

3. Secure all of the items to the inside of the box. Use all sides of the box. Some items may be suspended from the top using thread.

4. Make a list of the items on a separate sheet of paper.

5. Cover the entire box and leave an opening only large enough to allow an arm inside. An old sleeve of a sweater attached to the opening also works well. Label your touch box but do not tell what is inside.

In class, arrange all of the boxes so that no one can see inside them. Distribute paper and have each student try to identify and write down what is inside each box. Give extra credit for decorated boxes and for those with the most items that could not be identified.

Activity 14: Building Maslow's Hierarchy

Contributed by Jeanne Turner
Linn-Mar High School
Marion, Iowa

Ms. Turner has been teaching for 15 years at a large, suburban high school in the block format. She currently teaches Psychology I, Psychology II, and AP Psychology.

Students will apply their knowledge of the levels of Maslow's hierarchy to specific examples.

Building Maslow's Hierarchy

Materials Needed:

— Disposable plastic cups
— Large, thick rubber bands (3 1/2" x 1/2")
— String (cut into 2-foot strands)

Set-Up:*

Connect one side of six pieces of string around the rubber band. You will need this set up for every six students in the class, thus a class of 30 would need five rubber bands and 30 strings.

Each group of students will need 15 plastic cups:

> On five cups, write specific examples of items that would meet physiological needs.
> On four cups, write specific examples of items that would meet safety needs.
> On three cups, write specific examples to meet belongingness needs.
> On two cups, write specific examples to meet esteem needs.
> On one cup, write a specific example to meet self-actualization needs.

Directions:

— Students are placed in groups of four to six students.
— Each group gets a stack of 15 cups, one larger rubber band, and six strings. ("Need" examples should be mixed up within the stack.)
— Working in the group, each student should have to manipulate at least one string to pull open the rubber band. Working as a team, students must unstack their cups, read the examples, then create Maslow's hierarchy (putting the appropriate examples with the correct needs). (I usually have a student come to the front and help me model this format first.)
— Once all groups have their supplies, they race to see who can be the first team to correctly build their hierarchy.

Discussion:

Do you have any questions over the examples on the cups? What is the importance of the hierarchical structure?

---

* Depending on how much class time you want to spend, you can either have the students make these or make them yourself ahead of time. Once they are made, you can just save them for the next use.

Activity 15: Advertising: What Are They Trying to Sell You?

Contributed by Stacy La Ronge
Kewaskum High School
Kewaskum, Wisconsin

Ms. La Ronge has taught at Kewaskum High School for six years, and she can honestly say that she looks forward to coming to work every day. Her students are inspiring, and she feels an enormous sense of pride, seeing them grow and learn. She has taught Psychology for the full six years that she has been at Kewaskum; it has only been offered as an AP course for the past two years. Besides AP Psychology, Ms. La Ronge also teaches Human Relations, Sociology, and World Cultures. In a constant pursuit for the engaged learner, she is always looking for and developing activities for students. She feels it is essential that students see applicable uses for the information they learn.

Students often argue that advertising has no effect on them. They somehow believe that they are immune to its influence. This activity is intended to make students aware that not only are aspects of psychology applied to advertising but also that advertising affects our motivation and plays off of our emotions.

Advertising: What Are They Trying to Sell You?

Companies use various techniques to make their products seem desirable. We will be exploring how advertising is used to influence consumers by observing commercials, what they are advertising, and what methods are used. This will help us understand advertising's effect on the mind and behavior.

Each person will view one hour of television. During that time, students must record information on the following topics.

Type of programming: comedy, drama, animation, etc.

List of products being advertised and number of times they are advertised:

1.

2.

3.

4.

5.

6.

7.

8.

9.

10.

Target audience:

Methods of advertising (example: humor, thrill, fear, etc.):

Misleading information:

Effectiveness:

Obviously, billions of dollars would not be spent on advertising every year if it were not effective. Using the various concepts on motivation and emotion, explain why advertising is effective and how companies use it so that it has the greatest impact.

Activity 16: Stress Tug-of-War

Contributed by Margaret Davidson
L.V. Berkner High School
Richardson, Texas

Ms. Davidson teaches Introductory Psychology, AP Psychology, and Economics at L.V. Berkner High School in Richardson, Texas, where she has taught for 24 years. She was a participant and three-time presenter in the NSF Summer Institute for the Teaching of Psychology at Texas A&M University, served as lead teacher at the Arthur Vining Davis Foundation Psychology Teacher Institute at Nebraska Wesleyan University, and has presented numerous week-long College Board AP Psychology institutes. Ms. Davidson served as chair of Teachers of Psychology in Secondary Schools. She is a recipient of the Richardson Independent School District's RISE Award, *Who's Who Among America's Teachers*, and the Moffet Memorial High School Award from the American Psychological Association's Society of the Teaching of Psychology. She also received the College Board's Southwest Region Special Recognition Award in 2005.

As I introduce the topic of stress, I ask students to define stress and stressors. To visually show how small stressors can have a major impact on individuals' lives, I set up a tug-of-war.

Stress Tug-of-War

I gather a variety of materials for this demonstration. A typical list would include a length of lightweight nylon or cotton rope; a pair of gloves to protect the primary volunteer's hands; dolls to represent relationships; play money to represent money stressors; an empty pack of cigarettes and a representation of an alcoholic beverage to signify substance abuse or addiction; fast-food packaging to represent poor eating habits; cards to represent gambling; etc. Printed signs can also be used to represent many types of stressors in one's life.

The game of tug-of-war begins with the primary volunteer putting on gloves for protection and holding one end of the rope. Next, other students—who are holding the visual aids and/or signs to identify what stressors they represent—individually grab hold of the rope at the opposite end. With each additional student "stressor" giving a slight tug on the rope when he or she first grabs hold, it is easy to see how an individual could be overcome with stress. (As a cautionary note, I strongly remind students that this is a demonstration and not a true game of tug-of-war.)

In a follow-up activity, designated volunteers representing ways to cope with stress (diet, exercise, time management, relaxation, supporting relationships) help the primary volunteer with his/her end of the rope to balance life's stress.

The students then write a paper indicating their understanding of the types of stress, how stressors affect their lives, and healthy ways of dealing with stress.

Activity 17: Biodot Activity

Contributed by Jackie Mowery
Bayside High School
Virginia Beach, Virginia

Ms. Mowery has been teaching regular Psychology for 17 years and AP Psychology for three years. She currently teaches at Bayside High School in their Health Sciences Academy.

This activity involves the use of skin thermometers called Biodots. They are relatively inexpensive and easy to order. Students gain insight into their stress levels and love to see if they can change the color of their dots.

Biodot Activity

Concept:

Students will learn about the effects of stress on the body by wearing Biodot skin thermometers.

Objectives:

1. Explain the general adaptation syndrome.
2. Explain the relationship between stress, heart disease, and general health.
3. Compare the functions of the sympathetic and parasympathetic nervous systems.
4. Demonstrate the basic techniques of biofeedback.

Procedure:

1. Give each student a Biodot sticker and an accompanying card chart of color approximations for general interpretation of their current stress level. The darker colors represent higher stress levels in a person.

   Discuss the following questions:

   — What occurs during the three stages of the general adaptation syndrome?
   — Which part of the nervous system is activated during the first two stages?
   — What is the relationship between stress and skin temperature?
   — What could be the long-term effects of repeated activation of the sympathetic nervous system?

2. Ask students to concentrate on changing their Biodot color. If they show a relaxed state, ask them to concentrate on a stressful situation for a short period of time. If their dot reveals they are in a stressful state, ask them to visualize a pleasant, calm situation.

3. Discuss the role of the parasympathetic nervous system.

   Biodots may be ordered by phone, fax, or mail:

   Biodot of Indiana
   P.O. Box 1784
   Indianapolis, IN 46206
   1-800-272-2370
   Fax: (317) 635-7989

Activity 18: What Makes You Happier?

Contributed by Randy Ernst
Lincoln Public Schools
Lincoln, Nebraska

Mr. Ernst taught psychology at Lincoln High School, North Star High Schools, and Nebraska Wesleyan University. He is a co-author of the *National Standards for the Teaching of High School Psychology*, co-editor of the American Psychological Association's *Activities Handbook for the Teaching of Psychology (Vol. IV)*, and author of the College Board's *Teacher's Guide for Advanced Placement Psychology*. Randy has chaired the Teachers of Psychology in Secondary Schools (TOPSS) executive board, served on the College Board's AP Psychology Test Development Committee, and has been a table leader, question leader, and exam leader at the annual Advanced Placement Psychology Reading. He has authored or co-authored several TOPSS unit plans and has worked to infuse positive psychology across the K–12 curriculum. Mr. Ernst has provided in-service on the teaching of psychology to teachers around the United States and Canada and is an international psychology consultant for the College Board. Honors include Nebraska's 2006 Social Studies Educator of the Year Award, the National Association for the Advancement of Colored People's (Nebraska Chapter) 2004 Service to Children Award, and Time Warner's "Crystal Apple" National Teacher Award. Both the American Psychological Association and the University of Nebraska have recognized Mr. Ernst for excellence in teaching.

This wellness activity centers around positive-affect research on optimism and flow, which shows that activities that simply bring physical pleasure do not promote longer-lasting happiness, while activities that are rewarding and challenging do promote long-lasting happiness (Myers, 2004). When asked, my students often incorrectly predict that pleasurable activities bring more happiness than philanthropic endeavors.

What Makes You Happier?

Procedure:

Generate two lists in class. First, ask students to call out activities in which they have participated in the past week that were pleasurable. Second, ask students to identify activities they have participated in that were philanthropic. Follow this up with a discussion on how pleasurable and philanthropic activities differ.

Next, assign students to

A. Notice and write down the pleasurable and philanthropic activities they participate in over the next five days.
B. Note what kinds of positive emotions were elicited during each activity and how long the feelings lasted after the activity ended.
C. Hand in a paper noting the activities, emotions, and duration of the emotions. Students should also comment on the differences between the happiness derived from pleasurable vs. philanthropic activities. Discuss the findings after papers are handed in.

I first heard this activity explained by Martin Seligman to a group of students taking his positive psychology class. He suggested brainstorming a list of things to do for students who have trouble thinking of philanthropic activities. A list might include:

1. Serving those less fortunate at a soup kitchen
2. Doing things to help out around the house that you don't normally do
3. Helping a younger brother or sister with homework
4. Always holding the door open for those behind when entering a restaurant or school
5. Letting someone go in front of you when you're in line for lunch or at the grocery store, or merging with traffic

Discussion:

Students most often note that the positive emotions of philanthropic activities last longer than the emotions brought about by pleasurable activities. If not mentioned by students, I point out that the main difference between philanthropic and pleasurable activities is that the former benefits others while the latter benefits you. I close the discussion by mentioning how positive psychology research supports the notion that greater happiness is achieved when helping others rather than doing things that just benefit the self.

Reference:

Myers, D. G. (2004). *Research-based suggestions for a happier life*. Holland, Michigan: Hope College. Retrieved from the World Wide Web on May 12, 2007 at: http://www.davidmyers.org/Brix?pageID=48

Suggested Reading:

Seligman, M. E. P. (1998). *Learned optimism: How to change your mind and your life* (2nd. ed.). New York: Pocket Books.

Activity 19: Conservation of Liquid

Contributed by Charlie Blair-Broeker
Cedar Falls High School (Iowa)
Cedar Falls, Iowa

Mr. Blair-Broeker has taught psychology at Cedar Falls High School (Iowa) since 1978. He has been involved in a number of American Psychological Association (APA) initiatives, serving as a member of the task force that authored the "National Standards for High School Psychology," as chair of the executive board of Teachers of Psychology in Secondary Schools, and as co-editor of the fourth volume of the *APA Activities Handbook for the Teaching of Psychology*. For three years, Charlie co-directed Teaching the Science of Psychology, a summer institute for high school psychology teachers supported by the National Science Foundation and the Northern Kentucky University Foundation. He has been a rubric writer, table leader, or reader for AP psychology examinations since the test was first administered in 1992, completed a three-year term on the AP Psychology Test Development Committee, and is a psychology consultant for the College Board. Charlie has led dozens of teacher workshops across the United States and Canada. Among his teaching awards are the Grinnell College Outstanding Iowa Teacher Award, the University of Iowa Distinguished Teacher Award, and the APA Division 2 Teaching Excellence Award.

Children learn the concept of conservation as their cognitive skills develop. Jean Piaget demonstrated that 5-year-olds can be "tricked" into thinking that the amount of liquid increases as it is poured from a short, wide container into a tall, narrow one. They do not understand the fundamental basis of conservation, i.e., that the amount of something doesn't change because its shape does. One indication that children have moved from the preoperational stage of development to the concrete operational stage, which typically occurs around 6 years of age, is the mastery of conservation. This activity provides a very easy way for students to test children for the development of this skill.

Conservation of Liquid

Materials:

Each student will need two plastic beverage bottles with cone-shaped tops. Soda bottles work well. The labels should be removed, and each bottle should be filled to the same level (a good spot is where the cone shape begins right above the top of the label). The liquid should be colored so it is easily visible. The bottles should be tightly capped.

Procedure:

I usually demonstrate the use of the bottles in class and then allow students to take them home (I have several sets) to use with younger siblings, neighborhood kids, children at their house of worship, and so forth.

Begin with both bottles upright. Establish that they have the same amount of liquid. Then, turn one bottle upside-down and hold the two bottles side by side. Because of the cone, the fluid level is higher in the upside-down bottle than the right-side-up bottle. Ask the child, "Which bottle has more now?" Children who have not mastered conservation will say that the upside-down bottle contains more. Children who have mastered the concept will look at you bemusedly and wonder about your sanity for asking such a ridiculous question.

The preoperational child, of course, will think that the bottles hold the same amount again if you turn both bottles right side up.

Discussion:

During the next class period, I simply ask who tried the conservation task with children. Give several students an opportunity to describe the experience. They will respond with enthusiasm and provide examples of children who have and haven't learned conservation.

Activity 20: Piaget and Play-Doh

Contributed by Margaret Davidson
L.V. Berkner High School
Richardson, Texas

Ms. Davidson teaches Introductory Psychology, AP Psychology, and Economics at L.V. Berkner High School in Richardson, Texas, where she has taught for 24 years. She was a participant and three-time presenter in the NSF Summer Institute for the Teaching of Psychology at Texas A&M University, served as lead teacher at the Arthur Vining Davis Foundation Psychology Teacher Institute at Nebraska Wesleyan University, and has presented numerous week-long College Board AP Psychology institutes. Ms. Davidson served as chair of Teachers of Psychology in Secondary Schools. She is a recipient of the Richardson Independent School District's RISE Award, *Who's Who Among America's Teachers*, and the Moffet Memorial High School Award from the American Psychological Association's Society of the Teaching of Psychology. She also received the College Board's Southwest Region Special Recognition Award in 2005.

When discussing the various concepts and terms associated with Jean Paiget's theory of cognitive development, I get my students engaged in the lesson with Play-Doh. This activity offers an opportunity for students to gain a clear understanding of Piagetian theory, enhances the tactile learning method, and engages the class in the learning process.

Piaget and Play-Doh

I purchase a good number of small containers of Play-Doh. These containers can be used for a number of years with proper storage. The instructor may choose to mix up a batch of modeling clay from a recipe that is readily available on the Internet. I provide each group of two or three students with a container of Play-Doh or modeling clay. The group is instructed to make a representation of a term or concept from the Piagetian theory of cognitive development. This encourages them to use proper psychological terminology, to discuss the meaning of the terms, and to transfer knowledge from an oral or written input to a motor output.

An alternate suggestion is that the instructor assigns a stage of cognitive development for the groups to represent. If time permits, the groups could make a representation for each of Piaget's stages of cognitive development. Assessment is based on oral presentation and ability to explain the concept represented.

Typical examples include a modeled small toy and a blanket to cover it to explain object permanence; shaped letters or numbers to demonstrate use of symbolic language; a small ball of clay and a larger flattened clay shape to represent conservation; or designed religious symbols to represent abstract thought. Students report that this is an enjoyable activity that brings to mind their childhood years.

Activity 21: My Baby Book: A Record of Development

Contributed by Lindsay Hackman-Cushing
Buffalo Grove High School
Buffalo Grove, Illinois

Ms. Hackman-Cushing currently teaches AP Psychology at Buffalo Grove High School in the northwest suburbs of Chicago, Illinois. She received her bachelor's degree in social science secondary education from the Illinois State University in Normal, Illinois. In May 2006, she received her master's degree in the art of teaching and leadership from Saint Xavier University. She is currently working on a second master's degree in counseling and human services from Roosevelt University, Chicago. Additionally, Mrs. Hackman-Cushing serves as a co-chair for the Psychology Community sponsored by the National Council for Social Studies (NCSS) and co-hosts various pre-conference and conference instructional workshops each year at the NCSS annual conference. Mrs. Hackman-Cushing considers it an absolute honor to have assisted in the construction of this resource manual and hopes that new and experienced teachers find these teaching tips to be helpful.

"My Baby Book" is a project I assign in my Psychology 2 class, when I am teaching the unit on Development. While I cover most concepts in my textbook's two chapters on lifespan and development, I believe the construction of a baby book helps to further reinforce students' understanding of the chapters' most important concepts and people while making the topic really personal to them! The baby books I have received from former students have been beyond my expectations. Students usually spend between 15 and 30 hours constructing their books, and most of them look like they're professional enough to be sold in a store. Instead of simply learning about the various theories of development, students (and their families) can participate in a nostalgic trip down memory lane. It's a very memorable assignment. Students talk about it years after having taken my class, and new students ask eagerly for when the assignment is coming!

Note: Seldom, I have a student who was adopted, or who was born overseas and does not have early photographs, or who has lost both parents. In these situations, I tell the student to do the best he or she can. For example, in requirement #1, an adoptive mother cannot describe her pregnancy experience; instead, rather than skipping this item altogether, the student can describe (briefly) the adoption process or what it was like for the parents to meet their adopted baby for the first time. I make necessary alterations with individual students in person. In a worst-case scenario, I will offer the option of completing the baby book about a close friend or relative, if that's easier than making a personal baby book.

My Baby Book: A Record of Development

You will design and create a personal baby book that discusses many aspects of your personal development since day one! Follow the guidelines below (and exactly in this order) to create your baby book. You may use your mom, dad, or other family references to connect your past to the developmental concepts we will discuss in this unit. This is a *creative* assignment. Your baby book should not only contain personal and factual information, but it should also be decorative and unique to your personality. You should have a total of five pictures in your baby book. (I have placed them throughout the assignment below.) You should be creative, colorful, insightful, and careful of detail.

Section 1: Your General Fact Sheet(s)—Include graphics and detail wherever possible.

A. In one paragraph, describe your mom's pregnancy with you.

B. Why were you given your name?

C. What were the other names your parents were considering? Include both male and female names.

Section 2: Your Physical Development—Include graphics and detail wherever possible.

1. How long was your mom in labor?

2. What was your birth weight and length?

3. Photo: Include a baby picture taken of you at or right around birth.

4. How many months old were you when you learned to sit up?

5. How old were you when your first tooth came in?

6. How old were you when you took your first step?

7. When were you officially potty trained?

8. When did you lose your first tooth?

9. Compare your development for items #4, 5, and 6 with the averages. (Your book may be a good start.)

10. Create a timeline of the average brain development.

11. Discuss myelination and at which point you might personally be affected.

12. What is your current vision? (Do you have 20/20 vision? Do you wear glasses, contacts, etc.?)

13. At what age did you get glasses or contacts?

14. Define "puberty" (of course, in your own words!). Based on the characteristics of puberty, explain whether adolescence comes at a fixed age for all.

15. Photo: Include a picture of yourself around the age of puberty.

16. Make up and write a story about two friends (the same gender as you), one who is an early bloomer and one who is a late bloomer. How are their experiences different, better, or worse? What comes out of both of their experiences?

17. Draw up a "compare/contrast" list between males and females for all the physical changes in both genders' adult years. Define all terms, and provide results or consequences wherever appropriate.

Section 3: Your Language Development—Include graphics and detail wherever possible.

18. What was your first word?

19. When did you first say this word?

20. Why was this word your first?

21. Were there any funny sounds, words, and/or phrases you used to use?

22. If so, what were these sounds, words, and/or phrases supposed to mean?

23. Define telegraphic speech, overgeneralization, and overextension (in your own words).

(continued)

24. Did you use these forms of speech in any way? How? Provide examples.

25. Did you experience any language barriers during language formation (i.e., stuttering, lisps, etc.)?

26. Photo: Include a picture of yourself in the late-childhood years.

Section 4: Your Social-Emotional Development—Include graphics and detail wherever possible.

27. Who were you most attached to and why?

28. Define "imprinting" and explain whether this theory supports your attachment.

29. Were there any objects that you formed attachments with?

30. Were these attachments formed similar to Harlow's "contact comfort"? Why or why not? First, make sure to explain what "contact comfort" is.

31. Explain the overall effects of having no attachments in one's childhood. Include a personal example if you feel as though you fall into this category.

32. Photo: Include a picture from your early childhood years.

33. Summarize what adults experience, regarding later intimacy and attachment, as a result of the various infancy attachment levels.

Section 5: Your Cognitive Development—Include graphics and detail wherever possible.

34. Create or find a comic strip about an adolescent who is clearly in his/her early formal operational thinking stages. This should highlight the "personal fable" and "adolescent egocentrism" elements.

35. Admit to and explain, with your greatest humility, a specific time when you performed or experienced adolescent egocentrism, personal fable, and imaginary audience. (You know we all did, so go ahead and tell!)

Section 6: Your Moral Development—Include graphics and detail wherever possible.

36. Write a short paragraph explaining "where you are" regarding James Marcia's theory of development. For extra credit (five points), write a second paragraph explaining where your teacher is regarding James Marcia's theory of development. Make sure you explain why you think you (and your teacher) are placed specifically!

37. Photo: Include your most recent (late-adolescent) picture (i.e., senior picture?).

Section 7: Your Personality Development—Include graphics and detail wherever possible.

38. Look at the "temperament theory" and Thomas and Chess' temperament categories. Explain what type of child you were, based on this information. Give detail or examples.

39. Write a personal journal (one to two pages) about why stages #5 and #6 of Erikson's eight stages of personality development may be the highest hurdles to jump in life. Think about your junior high and high school years and what's to come in your post–high school years. Include physical, emotional, and cognitive aspects, and explain how these all fit into Erikson's stages #5 and #6.

This should be fun and easy to do as long as you budget your time appropriately. I guarantee I will be able to tell if this assignment was started and finished the night before it is due. Pace yourselves and have fun!

The Baby Book Grading Rubric

	GREAT 10-9 pts	GOOD 8-6 pts	AVERAGE 5-4 pts	FAIR 3-2 pts	POOR 1-0 pts
Section One: General Facts	All items are included, complete, and accurate	Most items are included, complete, and accurate	Half of all items are included, or all items are included but are incomplete/inaccurate	Few items are included and/or complete and accurate	Section is very incomplete, and info is inaccurate
Section Two: Physical Development	All items are included, complete, and accurate	Most items are included, complete, and accurate	Half of all items are included, or all items are included but are incomplete/inaccurate	Few items are included and/or complete and accurate	Section is very incomplete, and info is inaccurate
Section Three: Language Development	All items are included, complete, and accurate	Most items are included, complete, and accurate	Half of all items are included, or all items are included but are incomplete/inaccurate	Few items are included and/or complete and accurate	Section is very incomplete, and info is inaccurate
Section Four: Social-Emotional Development	All items are included, complete, and accurate	Most items are included, complete, and accurate	Half of all items are included, or all items are included but are incomplete/inaccurate	Few items are included and/or complete and accurate	Section is very incomplete, and info is inaccurate
Section Five: Cognitive Development	All items are included, complete, and accurate	Most items are included, complete, and accurate	Half of all items are included, or all items are included but are incomplete/inaccurate	Few items are included and/or complete and accurate	Section is very incomplete, and info is inaccurate
Section Six: Moral Development	All items are included, complete, and accurate	Most items are included, complete, and accurate	Half of all items are included, or all items are included but are incomplete/inaccurate	Few items are included and/or complete and accurate	Section is very incomplete, and info is inaccurate
Section Seven: Personality Development	All items are included, complete, and accurate	Most items are included, complete, and accurate	Half of all items are included, or all items are included but are incomplete/inaccurate	Few items are included and/or complete and accurate	Section is very incomplete, and info is inaccurate
Overall Facts	All facts are clear, correct, and appropriate	Most facts are clear, correct, and appropriate	Some facts are clear, correct, and appropriate; others are incorrect or unclear	Few facts are clear, correct, and appropriate	Facts are incorrect, inappropriate, and/or unclear
Overall Display	Your book looks very professional and creative	Your book is creative and organized	Your book is lacking creativity and/or organization	Your book is lacking time and effort	Your book was not given the creative time/attention
Overall Application	Perfect connections between you and all development information	Were able to make most information personally relevant	About half the required information was personally relevant	Few connections were made between information and your past	No connections made between your personal development and the assignment

COMMENTS:

SCORE: _____ / 100

Activity 22: Parenting Styles Skit

Contributed by Jimmy Stoverink
Jackson Senior High School
Jackson, Missouri

Mr. Stoverink graduated from Jackson High School in 1989. He then graduated from Southeast Missouri State University in 1993. He has been teaching high school social studies for the past 13 years. Although he has bounced around a bit, he is finally back at his alma mater (Jackson High School) teaching World History, Psychology, and AP Psychology. Although he has taught Psychology for 12 of his 13 years of teaching, this is his first year teaching AP Psychology. In addition to teaching, he also coaches cross-country and track. He is happily married and has two sons ages 11 and 17. Mr. Stoverink also owns his own restaurant, the Jackson Sports Grill.

I lead a class discussion about parenting styles in which I share examples from my childhood and my own experience as a parent. I also allow and encourage my students to share stories from their own experiences growing up. I teach that there are four parenting styles: authoritarian, authoritative, permissive indulgent, and permissive indifferent (I have found that some textbooks combine the last two into one parenting style just called permissive). This discussion takes the better part of one class period.

In the next class period, I have my students get into their cooperative learning groups, and I distribute the parenting styles skit handout. After each group performs a skit, I randomly call on students to identify which parenting style the skit represents and why they think so. I also ask if anybody disagrees, and this sometimes leads to a lively mini-debate. Sometimes, I ask students what a group could have done differently if the students in that group were supposed to depict a different parenting style.

I follow up the activity with a discussion about what the effects of different parenting styles might be, emphasizing how children of authoritative parents tend to be more confident of their morals and values and how they are more likely to identify with their parents. I make sure to emphasize that this is a correlational relationship and not necessarily a causal relationship.

Parenting Styles Skit

The way in which children seek independence and the ease with which they resolve conflicts about becoming adults depend in large part on the parent-child relationship. In class, we have discussed four different parenting styles. Your group's assignment is to create and perform a skit depicting one of those four styles.

Cast Members:

Grade scale: 5 = Obviously   4 = Mostly   3 = Kind of   2 = Not really   1 = Not at all

All members were involved in the creation and/or performance   _____ x 2 = _____

Creativity   _____ x 2 = _____

Audience (classmates/instructor) could easily identify parenting style   _____ x 2 = _____

Contains minimum of two scenes   _____

Total   _____ /35

Activity 23: Piaget's Preschool/Kindergarten Activity

Contributed by Judy Wong Taparra
Mililani High School
Mililani, Hawaii

Ms. Taparra graduated in 1983 from the University of Manoa with a bachelor's degree in education. She has worked for the Department of Education for more than 24 years. Ms. Taparra started teaching AP Psychology in the fall of 1999.

This activity takes a little coordination but is well worth the trouble. It is an excellent way to introduce your students to Piaget's cognitive development concepts and, at the same time, establish a working relationship with the elementary and preschool people in your community.

This project started my first year teaching AP Psychology. I had a friend who worked for a preschool based on our campus. I asked her if she would be interested in bringing her preschoolers to visit with my students. She was excited about it, and our students loved it. Since then, we have worked with her students, and this year we even had the kindergartners across the street participate in this project. Year after year, my students have reported in their class evaluations that working with the preschoolers was their favorite educational activity. Reading concepts from the book is one thing, but watching the book come alive is a learning experience they won't forget.

Basically, all I had to do was get approval from my principal, contact the teachers at the preschools around us, give them our schedule, work together finding a date, teach my students Piaget's concepts, demonstrate a practice lesson, and organize it so there is one preschool student to two high school students. I carefully planned my student's lesson with their preschoolers so they would purposefully cover Piaget's concepts. This particular activity has really helped my students to understand Piaget's concepts.

Attached are my worksheets that have evolved over time. They serve as a guide for my students while they interview their little visitors. To help decrease stranger anxiety, my students greet their youngsters with a star lei and then thank them later with a small gift bag that contains chips, cookies, bubbles, and a Mililani High School pencil.

If time permits, my students are assigned to create two report cards: one card with straight A's, which will be forwarded to their little student, and another card, which is submitted to me with their evaluation of their child's academic progress.

Piaget's Preschool/Kindergarten Activity

Child's name: _____   Age: _____

Concepts		Notes
Stranger Anxiety	How did your student react around unfamiliar people?	
Separation Anxiety	How did your student act when his/her teacher was not close by?	

Station	Directions	Comments
1.	Object permanence: Introduce two animals. Hide one of them under the towel. Ask, "Where did it go?"	
1.	Egocentrism: Place one animal on the left side of the binder. Ask… A. Can you see the *****? (Place another one on the right side.) B. Can you see the ****? C. Can they see each other? Why?	
2.	Symbolism: Ask… A. What's your favorite toy? B. What color is it?	
2.	Logic/Egocentrism: Ask… A How many brothers/sisters do you have? B. What are their names? C. How many brothers/sisters does _____ have?	
2.	Animism: Ask… A. Why does the sun get so hot? B. Why is the sky blue? C. Where does Santa Claus live?	
3.	Conservation: Number: Use 10 pennies and put them in two rows. Spread the bottom row. Ask: Does one row have more objects? Why?	
3.	Mass: Get two equal-sized Play-Doh balls. Roll one out. Ask: Do they have the same amount of Play-Doh? Why?	

(continued)

Station	Directions	Comments
3.	Volume: Get child to agree that two cups have same amount of water. Pour one into a taller cup. Ask: Do the two new beakers have the same amount of water? Why?	
3.	Length: Get two rulers and align them evenly next to each other. Ask: Are they the same length? Move one five inches to the right. Ask: Now which ruler is longer? Don't forget to ask why.	
3.	Area: Get the cow picture. Keep six squares together. Then spread another six squares around to the second cow. Ask which cow has more grass to eat. Ask why.	
4.	Orally ask: If you have one cookie and your mom gives you two more cookies, how many will you have? If you have three cookies and you give your dad one cookie, how many will you have left? Reversibility	
4.	Use the cookies...reversibility Be sure to let the child handle the cookies. Demonstrate: A. If you take two cookies, and I give you one more, how many cookies will you have? B. If you have two cookies and you ate one, how many will you have?	
5.	Moral development: Ask them to tell a story about the two pictures. Ask them which of the two got into more trouble. Ask why!	
6.	Hierarchical Classification: A. How many A? B. How many B? C. Which has more, A or C?	

Type a one-page reaction paper to describe what took place. Highlight, define, and apply three terms to today's activity. Would you agree or disagree with Piaget's cognitive development stages? Explain.

(continued)

MHS Report Card

_____
Child's Name

Grade	Description	Comments

MHS Report Card   A = Above level
                   C = At level
                   N = Needs Improvement (Below level)

_____
Child's Name

ID#: ____   Teacher: _____

ID#: ____   Note Taker: _____

ID#: ____   Note Taker: _____

Grade	Description	Comments
	Stranger Anxiety Separation Anxiety	
	Oral Reversibility or Concrete Reversibility	
	Object Permanence Animism	
	Conservation Number / Mass Volume / Length Area	
	Hierarchical Classification	

A. ID#: _____   Name: _____   [____]

B. ID#: _____   Name: _____   [____]

C. ID#: _____   Name: _____   [____]

Place a "T" in the [_____] above to indicate a Taparra's report card.

Place a "S" in the [_____] above to indicate a Student report card.

Activity 24: Bridging the Generation Gap: Interviewing a Senior Citizen About Adolescence

Contributed by Charlie Blair-Broeker
Cedar Falls High School (Iowa)
Cedar Falls, Iowa

Mr. Blair-Broeker has taught Psychology at Cedar Falls High School (Iowa) since 1978. He has been involved in a number of American Psychological Association (APA) initiatives, serving as a member of the task force that authored the "National Standards for High School Psychology," as chair of the executive board of Teachers of Psychology in Secondary Schools, and as co-editor of the fourth volume of the *APA Activities Handbook for the Teaching of Psychology.* For three years, Charlie co-directed Teaching the Science of Psychology, a summer institute for high school psychology teachers supported by the National Science Foundation and the Northern Kentucky University Foundation. He has been a rubric writer, table leader, or reader for AP psychology examinations since the test was first administered in 1992, completed a three-year term on the AP Psychology Test Development Committee, and is a psychology consultant for the College Board. Charlie has led dozens of teacher workshops across the United States and Canada. Among his teaching awards are the Grinnell College Outstanding Iowa Teacher Award, the University of Iowa Distinguished Teacher Award, and the APA Division 2 Teaching Excellence Award.

Students will learn about adolescence by interviewing senior citizens about their adolescence. This assignment helps students meet several objectives, including:

- Developing research skills (interview, case study)—Methods unit
- Applying lifespan principles to personal experience—Developmental unit

Bridging the Generation Gap: Interviewing a Senior Citizen About Adolescence

Assignment Guidelines:

- Arrange to conduct an informal interview (more like a conversation, really) with someone who is at least 65 years old. You may interview a relative, neighbor, or member of your house of worship. You may also call a nursing home to arrange to interview a resident. If you're having trouble finding someone to interview, contact me.

- Schedule at least 30 minutes to conduct the interview. Do not tape record the conversation (it makes people nervous), but do jot a few notes as you proceed. Have some topics for questions in mind before you go in, but be flexible and allow the conversation to follow its own course.

- The interview should be about adolescence as it was experienced by your interview subject. You may ask about school, friendship and dating activities, family, part-time jobs, and historical events (e.g., the impact of World War II or the Depression). You may also ask about your subject's opinions of today's teenagers and share your opinions as the conversation develops. The communication should be a two-way street.

- Prepare a two-page report about your interview. Rather than trying to summarize the whole conversation, restrict your paper to two to four topics that you found especially interesting or informative. Make sure you include your own well-reasoned opinions about each of the topics you highlight.

Activity 25: *Ordinary People*

Contributed by Susan Johnson
Oswego High School
Oswego, Kansas

O*rdinary People* is an excellent film to show during Development in Adolescence and/or Adulthood. Use the following sheet to stimulate critical thinking.

Ms. Johnson has taught Psychology at Oswego High School for the past 22 years and has been an adjunct instructor in Business and Psychology at Labette Community College for the past 26 years. Ms. Johnson received her bachelor's degree in education/business and her master's degree in counseling from Pittsburg State University. She is a National Board–certified counselor and is a member of Teachers of Psychology in Secondary Schools, Phi Kappa Phi, the American Counseling Association, and the Kansas Counseling Association. She received the Kansas School Counselor Association Outstanding School Counselor of the Year Award in 1998 and the Southeast Kansas Counseling Association Outstanding Counselor of the Year Award in 1996.

Ordinary People

Complete the sheet. Think your answers through carefully. Don't just write the most obvious answers—look below the surface for all the underlying feelings and causes. After you have completed this, the class will get in small groups for discussion, and then your insights will be shared with the class.

1. Why do you think Mom acted like she did?

   (Example answers: Her parents were very "surface" people, and she was the same way. She only wanted to show the "perfect" side, and her mother was the same way. Conrad reminded her constantly of her loss. She had never dealt with Buck's death—didn't cry, was afraid to love again because losing hurts too much, didn't want to face reality, etc.)

2. Why couldn't she handle "messes"?

   (Example answers: Then things weren't perfect and made her look bad. Her emotions were frozen inside and couldn't be let out, or she would break. Messes = imperfections. She probably had always had an easy, "perfect" life and didn't know what to do now. She was shallow and didn't want her friends to see that her family wasn't perfect. If everything went perfectly, then she wouldn't have to think or feel.)

3. Why did Dad act like he did?

   (Example answers: He liked to keep the peace, loved everyone, and wanted everyone to love each other. He let his wife keep him "going" but felt guilty about his feelings toward her. He didn't want to lose another son. He wanted to keep his family together and happy. He wanted to smooth things over for everyone. He really loved his son and didn't want to admit how cold his wife really was.)

4. Could you get any clues about Mom's reasons for her behavior from the little we saw of her parents?

(Example answers: They didn't talk about important things. They always kept a stiff upper lip. They kept up a good show because appearances were most important—"Jewish doctor? I thought we were through with all that." They ignored problems, too [like Conrad's profanity].)

5. Should we feel sorry for Mom? Why or why not?

(Example answers: Yes—she had locked all her feelings inside and was hurting a lot but trying to ignore it. Some day she would break and might not be able to put the pieces back together again—like the plate that she thought could be "saved"—and there would be no one there to help her through it. She was angry at both sons—one for dying and leaving her and the other for trying to kill himself. This was "who she was," and that image was breaking down.)

6. What did you think of the psychologist? What were some of the techniques he used?

(Example answers: He pretended to be Buck so Conrad could "yell it all out," confront him. He didn't answer all his questions; he let Conrad think them through. He did lots of probing and got Conrad mad so he would open up and quit saying how bad he was. He showed Conrad he cared about him. He said, "Feelings don't always tickle," and, "The point is not always to feel better." He used Conrad's anger to break him out. He was caring and said, "Feeling pain is better than nothing." When he asked Conrad what was the one wrong thing he did, Conrad responded, "I hung on"—that was the turning point.)

7. What did you think about Conrad's friend at school that tried to talk to him after the fight?

(Example answers: He was caring, concerned, and wanted to share his and Conrad's pain. He was a good friend and stuck up for Conrad. He had a good head on his shoulders.)

8. What were all the underlying causes of Conrad's suicide attempt?

(Example answers: He felt guilt that he lived, that his mother did not love him, anger at Buck—"all charm; tell me to fix things when it was too late." He didn't cry or acknowledge his feelings at the funeral. He felt responsible and angry that he held on and lived and Buck didn't. He was hurt and angry at Mom's attitude toward him. All the pain was swallowing him up like a hole. "I've got to get off the hook for what I did.")

9. Why did Mom leave? Will she come back?

(Example answers: She couldn't handle the "mess" of her life with Calvin, the loss of her husband's love, her family, and her "image." Calvin had kept them together, but now he had decided to be there for his son. "You're determined, but you're not strong." She couldn't tell Calvin she loved him—"I feel the same way about you I always have"—whatever that meant. She wouldn't be back unless she got psychiatric help, and that was doubtful. She was too proud and ran instead of trying to work things out.)

10. What will happen with the family now?

(Example answers: Conrad would continue to get therapy and learn to accept Mom and her frailties. Dad would probably only take her back if they could talk out Buck's death and her feelings for Conrad, but that was very doubtful. Dad and Conrad would grow stronger and closer and have a more honest relationship with them talking to each other.)

If you want, you could ask about Karen, i.e., what were some of the clues Karen gave that might lead you to believe she would kill herself? Possible answers: When she kept saying, "Everything is great," and kept repeating herself but didn't really realize it. When she said, "Let's have a great Christmas, great year, great rest of our lives," she was trying too hard. She was too effusive, wouldn't talk about the time in the hospital, etc.

Activity 26: Personality Timeline

Contributed by Susan Johnson
Oswego High School
Oswego, Kansas

Ms. Johnson has taught Psychology at Oswego High School for the past 22 years and has been an adjunct instructor in Business and Psychology at Labette Community College for the past 26 years. Ms. Johnson received her bachelor's degree in education/business and her master's degree in counseling from Pittsburg State University. She is a National Board–certified counselor and is a member of Teachers of Psychology in Secondary Schools, Phi Kappa Phi, the American Counseling Association, and the Kansas Counseling Association. She received the Kansas School Counselor Association Outstanding School Counselor of the Year Award in 1998 and the Southeast Kansas Counseling Association Outstanding Counselor of the Year Award in 1996.

I ask students to create a timeline of their life to the present and write an analysis of their personality using the information they gathered for their timeline.

Personality Timeline

Directions:

1. Complete a timeline of your life to the present. The following is a short example:

   1965 — Born in Joplin, MO; 8 lb 2 oz; 21.5 inches; no complications

   1970 — Had tonsils removed at KU Medical Center while Dad was in the same hospital
   having treatments for cancer
   Started kindergarten; first kiss and first boyfriend

   1971 — Tested for gifted—very scared

   1972 — Dad died Christmas Eve; Christmas presents from many townspeople
   Afraid to leave my Mom

2. Now add in events going on in the world, state, or community (examples: 9/11, Iraq War, NCLB)

3. Analyze your timeline, keeping in mind things in your life that may have affected you, such as:

   - divorce in the family
   - moving houses, schools, or states
   - death in the family
   - births
   - hospitalizations
   - break-ups with boyfriends/girlfriends
   - loss of best friend
   - disability
   - money struggles
   - academic struggles
   - parents fighting; parents fighting with siblings
   - job/no job/can't find job
   - very personal things (examples: legal, sexual, drugs/alcohol)
   - accomplishments in school or athletics

   Some things to think about:

   ○ feel successful?
   ○ outgoing or shy?
   ○ family oriented?
   ○ do OK in school?
   ○ have always felt smart/dumb/so-so/etc.?
   ○ feelings about yourself?
   ○ goals?
   ○ worried about the future?
   ○ hobbies?

   Other issues:

   ✦ sense of initiative?   ✦ sense of identity?
   ✦ sense of industry?   ✦ sense of intimacy?

4. Write an analysis of your personality using the information you have gathered and answered above. Attach your timeline to your paper.

Activity 27: Death: An Ending or a Transition?

Contributed by Rob Nelson
Shorewood High School
Shorewood, Washington

Dr. Nelson's life experiences have included teaching World Geography and Social Psychology for the Shoreline School District in the state of Washington for the past 30 years. Dr. Nelson has traveled in Europe, Africa, Central America, Micronesia, and Asia. He lived overseas for the better part of 20 years and completed high school at the American Academy in Athens, Greece. He also served four years in the U.S. Navy with two tours in Vietnam. Dr. Nelson has studied post-secondary education and received his master's and doctorate degrees in adult education and the Running Start program.

This activity helps to teach students to think outside of the box with regard to social contemporary issues. Death is an everyday fact. Thinking about it is one thing, but asking students to talk openly about what's really troubling them about death can be difficult. We, as educators, may help students feel "OK" and that they aren't alone with their feelings.

Death: An Ending or a Transition?

In writing, please answer the questions on your own. One-word answers will not be enough. Give a reason/explanation for your answer.

1. Define "death."

2. Do you believe in an "afterlife" of some kind? Yes, no, maybe? Why or why not? If you answered yes or maybe: what can/could the afterlife be like, and what do you need to do in your earthly life to get there?

3. After a death, what are some purposes of having a funeral?

4. How does your family plan a funeral to meet these purposes? What are some of the rituals used in dealing with death?

5. At what age should children be allowed or encouraged to attend funerals? What could be some of the benefits or harms? Explain.

6. If you could know the exact month, day, and year of your death, would you want to know? Why or why not?

Activity 28: Who Are You?

Contributed by Rachel Fitzgerald
Faribault High School
Faribault, Minnesota

This is **Ms. Fitzgerald's** third year teaching Introductory Psychology and AP Psychology, as well as Sociology and World History, at her alma mater, Faribault High School. St. Olaf College is where she received her undergraduate degree in social studies education. She just completed her master's degree through Southwest Minnesota State University after presenting her research paper and portfolio. Teaching and psychology are her two passions, and she feels so fortunate to have the opportunity to have a career that combines the two.

I have students examine and reflect on their personalities by decorating the inside of a box with their inner ideas and values and the outside of the box with how they appear to others. This concept also ties in with ideas from adolescent identity development and social psychology. This assignment leads to many great discussions on what personality consists of, as well as personality development, self-awareness, and self-image. It works well as an introduction to the Personality unit or as a culminating activity.

Depending on how you cover personality, you could alter this assignment and the requirements in a variety of ways. You could have the students have each "wall" of the inside of the box represent a psychologist or one of the major personality perspectives (trait, psychoanalytic, etc.). They would then decorate that wall to correspond with how that perspective would view their personality or the formation of their individual personality. For example, for psychoanalytic, they might put in photographs of their childhood or icebergs to represent the subconscious; for the learning/behaviorist perspective, they might put up media images, role models, rewards, etc. Students could also pick the perspective with which they most agree and use that as a basis for creating or decorating their box.

Who Are You?

How do others view you?

How do these views differ?

Why do they differ?

Directions:

Create a box. The inside of the box should represent who you think you are. The outside of the box should represent how you think others view you or how you represent yourself to the world.

Steps:

1. Find a box of any size. (Remember: We will need to see the inside, so no lids.)
2. Decorate the box. The inside of the box should represent your "true self," your inner thoughts, goals, and personality. The outside of the box should reflect how you believe others view you and/or the image that you project to the rest of the world.
3. Prepare a brief written description of the inner and outer personalities. Also, explain why and how these are similar and different.

Activity 29: "Frasier's Edge"

Contributed by Kelly A. Cavanaugh
Career Center
Winston-Salem, North Carolina

Ms. Cavanaugh has been teaching AP Psychology since 2002 and has been the online course instructor/developer since 2004. She received her bachelor's degree in psychology from Dartmouth College and her master's degree in liberal studies from the University of North Carolina at Greensboro.

This activity is done while viewing an episode of the television show *Frasier* (Season 8, Episode 12). This episode is about Frasier receiving a lifetime achievement award and the issues that he has as a result. There are many Freudian terms mentioned and multiple examples of defense mechanisms.

"Frasier's Edge"

The students have already learned what the defense mechanisms are. While viewing the episode, the students are asked to find two examples of each defense mechanism. They should also write down five examples of other Freudian terms that are used.

Before starting the video, it is helpful to give examples of some things that the students might be looking for: an adult acting like a child could be an example of regression, or a person overcompensating for his or her feelings in an obvious way is an example of reaction formation. There are plenty more instances in the episode than the students are required to write down, but they will need to pay attention so that they don't miss some!

Activity 30: Trait Perspective of Personality

Contributed by Kimberley Sinclair

Glendale High School
Glendale, California

This year, **Ms. Sinclair** is teaching Psychology for the first time. She has taught Health for the past 14 years. She has a professional clear in health science and a supplemental authorization in psychology. Ms. Sinclair received a master's degree in public health from the University of California, Los Angeles, in June of 2005. In September of 2002, she retired from the U.S. Army Reserve as a major.

Before we begin, I have my students take a Jung typology test online at http://www.humanmetrics.com/cgi-win/JTypes2.asp. In addition, students should already have an understanding of the trait perspective of personality before doing this assignment.

Trait Perspective of Personality

Students will write a five-paragraph autobiography about themselves using the trait perspective of personality.

It is best to demonstrate examples from your own life so that students can see that they must have evidence to back up the traits they are claiming to have. I also give my students a list of trait words so that they have something to reference. I tell them they must be positive words.

The students should include the following in their essays: an introduction of trait perspective, one trait the student got from his or her father, one trait from his or her mother, one trait from experience, one trait that is unique to the student, and a conclusion.

I gave them one week to write their essays. It takes two class periods to explain the trait perspective and give examples. It makes for interesting reading and may satisfy your school-wide instructional writing focus, if you have one.

Activity 31: Classical Conditioning: Pupil Dilation

Contributed by Whitney Blankenship
Leander High School
Leander, Texas

Ms. Blankenship is currently in her 13th year with the Leander Independent School District in Leander, Texas. Over the years, she has taught World Geography, U.S. History, International Baccalaureate History of the Americas, and International Baccalaureate Psychology, as well as AP U.S. History and Pre-AP World Geography. In May 2005, she was named a regional finalist for H-E-B's Excellence in Education Award. She is working on her doctorate in social studies education at The University of Texas at Austin.

I have used this activity every year to allow students to see for themselves the effects of classical conditioning. I also use it as a review of the concepts of neutral, unconditioned, and conditioned stimuli and responses after introducing classical conditioning. Students are skeptical at first, but they are always thrilled when it "works." The experiment also gives them a personal experience they can use to enhance their recall of the concepts involved. I often refer back to the experiment throughout the Learning unit to draw attention to the similarities and differences between classical conditioning, operant conditioning, and observational learning.

Classical Conditioning: Pupil Dilation

To do this experiment, all you need is a room that is relatively dark when the lights are out and a bell, buzzer, or similar noise device. It takes 10 to 15 minutes to complete.

After introducing Pavlov's classical study of dog salivation, along with the major concepts, I tell students that we are now going to classically condition their pupils to dilate when the lights are on and I ring a bell. I remind them that for this to work, they are going to need to be quiet so that they can hear the bell. I tell them that it will take roughly 30 to 35 trials for it to work, so they need to be patient. I then turn the lights off, wait a second or two so that their eyes will start dilating, and then I ring the bell. The lights are then turned back on, and the process is repeated. As we approach the last trial, I have students pair up with another student so that they can look at each others' eyes (some students like to use a mirror so they can see their own pupils). After the last trial, I tell students to watch their partners' pupils, and then I ring the bell without turning off the light. I usually get around a 90% success rate the first time.

After the experiment is concluded, we run through each of the steps, and students identify the neutral, unconditioned, and conditioned stimuli and responses. They also determine the type of pairing that was used (short delayed, simultaneous, etc.). We then discuss the concept of extinction, and I ask students to predict what percentage of the students will experience pupil dilation the following class period. At the beginning of each class, for the next week, students pair up, and I ring the bell. We then track the time it takes for the behavior to be extinguished in the entire class.

If you have time, you can also demonstrate higher-order conditioning by pairing the bell with a new stimulus.

Adapted from:
Lessons in Psychology. Portland, ME: J. Weston Walch, Publisher, 1985.

Activity 32: Mental Imagery

Contributed by Ann Boline
Maple Grove Senior High School
Maple Grove, Minnesota

Ms. Boline is a social studies teacher and has been teaching Psychology and AP Psychology at Maple Grove Senior High School for 10 years. She has her undergraduate degree in social sciences and education from Gustavus Adolphus College and a graduate degree in social science (family education) from the University of Minnesota.

Classical conditioning is a difficult concept to introduce to students who have never been exposed to it before. I find this exercise is a good anticipatory set for the classical conditioning lesson. After this exercise has been completed, it is easy to refer to when discussing the key concepts of classical conditioning.

Mental Imagery

Equipment Needed:

CD player and a CD of music from the movie *Jaws*. (You can also play the music from the *Jaws* DVD.)

Objective:

Students will be introduced to the concepts of classical conditioning and involuntary bodily response.

Lesson Direction:

When students come into the room, have them put their heads down on their desks and tell them to relax. I usually have the lights dimmed, too.

Read the following mental imagery slowly: Imagine that it is a hot summer day. You are on the beach with your friends. The waves are crashing down onto the white sand, and the smell of salt water looms in the air. The sun is scorching. You are lying on the sand with the sun beating down on your face. You are getting hotter and hotter and can stand it no longer. You and your friends run toward the ocean, splashing in the shallow water. The water cools your feet, and you instantly feel a sense of relief from the blazing sun. You notice other people engaging in similar activity around you. You notice the shallow waters are packed full of people of all ages, enjoying the summer heat and the cool ocean water. You see people splashing in the water, playing in the waves, laughing, talking. You begin to swim out a bit deeper to separate from the noise, and you relax as you feel the coolness of the water refresh your body more and more. You swim completely underneath the water and taste salt on your lips as you emerge from below the surface. As you swim and float in the water, the feel of sand beneath your feet slowly begins to disappear. The chatter and laughter from before becomes more of a murmur as you move further from shore. You completely enjoy the peaceful, quiet, refreshing surroundings as you float in the calm ocean water…

As soon as you say the last word ("water"), press "play" on the CD player. Slowly the *Jaws* music will begin. Students will start to snicker, open their eyes, and a few may even raise their heads.

After the music has played, restore the lights and ask students what just happened. Ask what state their bodies were in before the music played and what state their bodies were in after the music played (they should give specific examples, like heart started racing, breathing faster, etc.). Why?

Introduce the concept of classical conditioning. Stress how this conditioning is involuntary and involves the body's reaction to a situation (demonstration: music associated with the dangerous situation of a shark).

I usually go into the lecture of classical conditioning at this point and refer to this demonstration throughout the lecture.

Activity 33: Dotting Exercise

Contributed by Polly Patrick
Minnetonka High School
Minnetonka, Minnesota

Ms. Patrick has taught English, Social Studies, and Psychology for more than 30 years. Since coming to Minnetonka High School in Minnesota, she has taught psychology at every level, including AP, International Baccalaureate, General, and classes for at-risk students. Ms. Patrick uses a variety of activities and technology to help her students learn the concepts of psychology. Her classes are only a semester in length, so the need for quick engagement is critical!

Quick activities grab the students' attention and help them engage in the topic. The following activity does that and provides a clear model for being able to examine the concept of classical conditioning.

Dotting Exercise

Use: Introduces the concept of classical conditioning

Materials: Paper and pen for each participant
 Clock/watch with a second hand for timing

Time: 5 minutes

This activity works well for any size group.

Directions:

1. Invite the class to participate in an experiment to see if they can learn "faster finger dexterity" by participating in five timed trials. "Play with it" in your presentation to pique their curiosity.

2. Instruct the class to number their paper in the following pattern:

       1   2

             3

       4   5

   Instruct them to space the numbers to allow room for many "dots" around each number for each of the five trials.

3. Announce that you will be giving the class five 5-second trials. During each trial, participants are to put as many dots as possible around the number on their paper that corresponds to a given trial. Illustrate on the white board by putting as many dots as you can around the number "1" in several seconds, just to give them the idea visually.

                .. ..
             .. ..
   Example: .. . . . 1 . . . . .
                .. . .

   (Dots will be randomly placed all around the number.)

4. Have a watch or clock ready with a second hand for timing.

5. Now check to see if the students are "ready." Instruct them not to begin until you say, "Go."

6. When you say, "Go," stomp your foot and clap your hands all at the same time.

7. Call out, "Stop," at the end of 5 seconds.

8. After completing the first time trial, walk around the room among the students as though you care a lot about checking for the number of dots. Praise the students for their efforts.

9. Call time for trial 2 using the same process as you used for the first trial: Call out, "Go," stomp your foot, and clap your hands.

10. After you call, "Stop," this time, ask them to look for their own progress, saying, "Don't count, but do you see your progress?" Get some brief feedback. Then continue.

11. Have them prepare to begin trial 3. This time ask if they are ready and look as though you are timing the trial the same way as in the first two trials. But do not say, "Go." Just stomp your foot and clap your hands and begin timing.

12. Many of the students will begin making dots even though you didn't say, "Go." Let them keep going for a bit. Then stop and note that, "Some of you began making dots even though I didn't say, 'Go.' Why do you suppose that's true? We call this conditioning. We'll come back to this question shortly. Thank you for participating!" The participants have been "conditioned" (to begin with their dots) in response to your stomping and clapping.

13. Debrief them either now or after you cover Pavlov's work. Discuss with the students the definition and process of classical conditioning.

Activity 34: Clicker Training

Contributed by Kelly A. Cavanaugh
Career Center
Winston-Salem, North Carolina

Ms. Cavanaugh has been teaching AP Psychology since 2002 and has been the online course instructor/developer since 2004. She received her bachelor's degree in psychology from Dartmouth College and her master's degree in liberal studies from the University of North Carolina at Greensboro.

To demonstrate techniques of operant conditioning, use a dog clicker (available at any pet store) to condition a student into doing a predetermined behavior whenever he/she hears the clicker. This conditioning can be further reinforced by initially providing an edible treat to be associated with the clicker sound.

Clicker Training

Choose a student volunteer who is outgoing and not afraid to try new things in front of other students! The student volunteer is asked to step outside. While the student is outside, the activity is explained to the rest of the class, and the class chooses the specific action the volunteer is to do. Past examples include standing on a chair to sing the National Anthem to the flag, resetting the clock to a specified time, writing a piece of personal information on the whiteboard, retrieving an item from a particular student's book bag, etc. The behavior should not be obvious, yet it should be one that can be directed to a specific location in the room and then shaped as the student tries various behaviors.

Be sure to instruct the rest of the class not to give any feedback, verbal or otherwise. The class will be unable to hold back at points, and any unintentional cues they give the volunteer will serve as a good post-activity discussion.

Invite the student back in. Do not give the student any verbal directions, except to say, "We have chosen a behavior we would like you to do. I will let you know when you have gotten it right." The student will be very puzzled, but that's okay!

For the short version, stand next to the student, click the clicker, and provide an edible treat (M&M's or Skittles work well). Do this a few times until you feel the student understands that the clicker means he/she will get a treat.

For the long version (about a class period or 40 minutes), do not give the student any indication initially that you have the clicker. As the student wanders the room, use the clicker to encourage him/her toward the specific location. The student will not understand the clicker at first but will soon learn from the class's reactions that the clicker means "you're getting warmer." (For the short version, each click should be followed initially by an edible treat. Eventually you will scale back to a variable-ratio schedule.)

Continue shaping the behavior. Soon the volunteer will understand the location but not yet the behavior. Then the shaping will only be required for the behavior attempts until the student achieves the desired behavior.

Activity 35: Operant Conditioning: Gambling Experiment

Contributed by Stacy La Ronge
Kewaskum High School
Kewaskum, Wisconsin

Ms. La Ronge has taught at Kewaskum High School for six years, and she can honestly say that she looks forward to coming to work every day. Her students are inspiring, and she feels an enormous sense of pride, seeing them grow and learn. She has taught psychology for the full six years that she has been at Kewaskum; it has only been offered as an AP course for the past two years. Besides AP Psychology, Ms. La Ronge also teaches Human Relations, Sociology, and World Cultures. In a constant pursuit for the engaged learner, she is always looking for and developing activities for students. She feels it is essential that students see applicable uses for the information they learn.

Through this exercise, students see firsthand how reinforcement affects behavior. They can repeat the procedures a number of times by switching decks. It's also interesting to see how their experience with the previous deck affects their betting with the next deck. Concepts from the Memory and Cognition units could also be tied into this.

Operant Conditioning: Gambling Experiment

Procedures:

1. Divide students into pairs. Designate one person as the dealer and the other as the gambler.

2. Hand each pair of students a deck of cards and some candy Skittles. Hand out enough Skittles so that students can wager and win. Set up the decks as follows:

   a. Fixed ratio: every third card is a winner

   b. Variable ratio: approximately every fifth card is a winner (should average to five)

   c. Extinction: first five cards are winners, and then no more

   d. Partial: random winners for the first 15 cards, and then no more

   e. No reinforcement: no winning cards

3. Have students bet on whether a heart is going to be turned over. Have them only bet one amount. If the heart is turned over, they receive double the number of Skittles they bet. If there is not a heart, they lose their Skittles. They must bet each time to play. They may quit the game and walk away with their Skittles at any time.

4. Afterwards, have the students guess which type of reinforcement was being used. Allow students to compare how their behaviors differed depending on the type of reinforcement. Discuss the following issues:

   a. What determined if they continued to bet or how much they bet?

   b. If they stopped betting, why did they stop?

   c. How did they feel while gambling? Why did they feel that way?

Activity 36: Portfolio of Key Theories in Learning

Contributed by Barbara Pester

Lincoln North Star High School
Lincoln, Nebraska

Ms. Pester has been a teacher of psychology at North Star High School in Lincoln, Nebraska, for three years. In addition, she is an adjunct faculty member in the Human Services Division at Southeast Community College. She is also a member of Teachers of Psychology in Secondary Schools, an AP reader for the Educational Testing Service, and a member of the National Council for the Social Studies.

I have my students create a portfolio of the key concepts of learning. This is an activity that allows the student to apply learning concepts to a variety of media sources.

Portfolio of Key Theories in Learning

The following components must be included in your portfolio. Each component is worth 10 points for a total of 60 points.

1. Pavlov's Classical Conditioning
2. Watson's Little Albert Experiment
3. Principles of Conditioning
4. Schedules of Reinforcement
5. Reinforcement and Punishment
6. Observational Learning

— For each category above, you are expected to design portfolio entries that concisely illustrate key theories, concepts, vocabulary, and major theorists. These entries must be visually appealing and must be detailed in their summaries.

— Copying or scanning visuals from the text or the Internet is not allowed. Clip art is acceptable. You can use magazines or draw your own pictures. Create graphic organizers or charts. Use your imagination!

— Consider this as your guide: When it comes time for the AP test, will what you have included as the summary be enough for you to remember the details of the study or theory? Does making the visual help you organize the information in your "brain files"? Writing one or two sentences is NOT enough; an entire page of summary is more than necessary. Capture the essence and use the visuals and/or graphics to portray and/or cement information.

Activity 37: Pictographs

Contributed by Whitney Blankenship
Leander High School
Leander, Texas

Ms. Blankenship is currently in her 13th year with the Leander Independent School District in Leander, Texas. Over the years, she has taught World Geography, U.S. History, International Baccalaureate History of the Americas, and International Baccalaureate Psychology, as well as AP U.S. History and Pre-AP World Geography. In May 2005, she was named a regional finalist for H-E-B's Excellence in Education Award. She is working on her doctorate in social studies education at The University of Texas at Austin.

Over the years, I have often struggled to make essential vocabulary a little less boring for students—not exactly an easy task. Research indicates that one of the best ways to strengthen recall of information is multiple encoding. By incorporating a term and its definition into a pictorial format, students' recall is enhanced. Several years ago, I began to use pictographs as a way for students to apply their vocabulary knowledge in a creative way. Essentially, students are using the letters in a vocabulary word to create a picture that illustrates the meaning of the term—for instance, writing the word "tiny" in very small letters, or the word "tall" in long, skinny letters.

Once they understand what they are being asked to do, students can be very creative. For example, this past year, some students depicted the letters in "psychodynamic" as the blood vessels in the brain. If you just look at the poster, it appears to be a drawing of a brain; however, if you look more closely, you can see that the blood vessels actually spell "psychodynamic"—alluding to the idea of the unconscious mind.

I have used this technique for everything from simple vocabulary to broader concepts, and it works well with both. Although I have used the activity as a review before tests, with students presenting their creations, it can easily be simplified into an individual exercise.

Pictographs

Because I am using this as a review activity, I divide the class into pairs, assigning each pair a perspective (biological, cognitive, behavioral, etc.) or a psychological subfield (social, evolutionary, developmental, etc.).

After each team has its assigned term, the assignment is introduced, and I show the class numerous examples from past years. However, I tell them that they must be original in their design, they cannot copy a previous year's poster, and the only words on the poster should be the term itself. The picture must represent the definition and make it obvious to the viewer what the definition is.

Students are given newsprint and art supplies and have 30 to 45 minutes to complete their poster. After all of the posters have been completed, each group presents its poster to the class and explains the reasoning behind the pictograph, using appropriate psychological terminology. The posters are then displayed around the room as a quick reference throughout the year.

Variation: Have students create a vocabulary journal with each page divided into two columns (or they can use note cards that can be put on a ring for easy study). In one column (or on the front of the note card), they write the definition of the term; in the second column (or on the back of the note card), they draw a picture to illustrate the term. They can easily study the information for the test by folding the paper in half (or flipping the note cards) and using the pictures to stimulate their recall of a definition.

Sources:

Marzano, Richard J. "Nonlinguistic Representations." *Classroom Instruction That Works: Research-Based Strategies for Increasing Student Achievement*. Alexandria, VA: Association for Supervision and Curriculum Development, 2001.

Whitson, Deborah. "Bringing World War II Terms to Life." *World War II*. Palo Alto, CA: Teachers' Curriculum Institute, 1991.

Activity 38: Memory/Hemispheric Specialization Experiment

Contributed by Beth Ferns
Hudson High School
Hudson, Massachusetts

Ms. Ferns has been a teacher for 16 years, with six years at the middle school level and 10 years at the high school level. She presently teaches AP Psychology, General Psychology, Honors and regular Contemporary Legal Issues, and Honors Criminology as part of the online Virtual High School. She is a National Board–certified teacher in high school social studies. She is also an adjunct faculty at Lesley University in Cambridge, Massachusetts, in the graduate education department and at Southern New Hampshire University where she teaches in the education and sociology departments. Ms. Ferns has both a bachelor of science degree and a master of science degree in criminal justice with a specialization in forensic criminology. She also has a master's degree in education. In her spare time, Ms. Ferns enjoys spending time on her family's boat with her husband, three children, two stepchildren, and her mother. She loves to read and, when time permits, to catch episodes of *Law & Order* and *CSI*. She follows the Red Sox and Patriots faithfully. Ms. Ferns would also like to acknowledge the collaboration of her former student intern, Alexandra Agrillo, in the development of this lesson.

In this activity, students utilize the concepts of hemispheric specialization of the brain and short-term memory. Using the idea that, depending on brain dominance, people will recognize either faces or words/numbers better, students test subjects with a self-made memory game. Subjects are asked to complete a questionnaire about hand dominance and traits. Students analyze the results for patterns between memory and traits as they compare them to hand (hemispheric) dominance.

Memory/Hemispheric Specialization Experiment

The purpose of this project is to examine the connection between hemispheric specialization and memory. According to research on hemispheric specialization, the right side of the brain recognizes faces, places, and objects, and the left side recognizes words, letters, and numbers. Given this fact, should people with specific brain dominance remember certain objects better than others? To examine this question, you will follow the requirements listed below.

Requirements:

1. Students may work in groups of three or four people.

2. Students should make memory experiment cards:

   a. eight pairs of matching cards with faces on them

   b. eight pairs of matching cards with words on them

3. If you are working in a group of three, you must test four people each. If you are working in a group of four, you must test three people each. There should be a total of 12 people tested for your group.

4. The experiment

   a. Create two sets of 16 cards. Each set should have eight identical pairs. One set should be faces, and the other should be printed words.

   b. Choose subjects of different ages. You should have an equal number of subjects from the following age groups: under 12, 13–21, 21–40, over 40 years.

   c. Place the cards face down and ask subjects to turn them over one at a time to match the cards. When the cards have been matched, remove them from the pile. You may either time each trial or count the number of matches needed to complete all eight matches.

   d. Subjects should do this matching exercise for both sets of cards.

   e. After each subject has completed the trials, have the subject fill out the questionnaire. Be sure to carefully track the results of the matching with the answers given on the sheet.

5. The data

The results should be presented with your analysis and graphic data. Each person should choose one aspect of the experiment to analyze and graph the results.

6. The analysis

   a. Students may report their results in an oral presentation. Graphs may be done on a poster board, overhead transparencies, or PowerPoint slides.

   b. Each student must participate in the preparation and sharing of the results.

   c. Compare the results of the memory tests with the results of the surveys.
      i. What are the overall results? How does the matching of cards compare to the results of the questionnaires?
      ii. Each person in the group should examine a specific aspect of the research, i.e., differences in age, differences in gender, differences between specific traits/skills and memory results.
      iii. Identify any confounding variables that may have influenced results.

   d. Create an oral presentation that summarizes your findings.

   e. Each person must create a graph that clearly represents his/her results.

Subject # _____ Age of subject _____ Gender _____

Please check off the answers that you feel are applicable.

1. I perform most tasks with my _____ hand.

2. The following traits describe me (check off all that apply):

   _____ sociable   _____ reserved   _____ optimistic
   _____ pessimistic   _____ sad   _____ cheerful
   _____ logical   _____ creative   _____ analytical
   _____ emotional   _____ stressed   _____ self-confident

3. I believe that I have strength in the following areas (check all that apply):

   _____ mathematics   _____ writing   _____ problem solving
   _____ reading maps   _____ drawing   _____ communication
   _____ remembering faces   _____ remembering words
   _____ arranging things in an order
   _____ arranging things in a pattern

Memory Testing Results

Subject # _____   Age_____   Gender_____

Faces

Number or amount of time needed to complete matching

_____

Numbers

Number or amount of time needed to complete matching

_____

Activity 39: High School Show and Tell

Contributed by Michael McLane
Sterling Heights High School
Sterling Heights, Michigan

This is a very good activity to do toward the end of the semester. It is especially nice for the students who are graduating. Often, when students graduate, they only reflect back on their senior year. The goal of this activity is to have the students reflect back on their entire educational career by applying the semantic network model of long-term memory.

After graduating from Eastern Michigan University over nine years ago, **Mr. McLane** returned to his high school alma mater to follow in the footsteps of his mentor, Dan Bolla. For the past nine years, he has been a faculty member at Sterling Heights High School and has worked to build a strong psychology program. His goal was to continue to develop an already popular psychology program. In addition to the General Psychology class he was teaching, he implemented AP Psychology and developed another course entitled Transitional Psychology. He also coaches his high school golf team and loves traveling to Northern Michigan with his wife and golden retriever.

High School Show and Tell

Directions:

- Students are asked to bring in one item from any past school year. They are instructed that they will only show the item at first to the class. They will not say anything about the item until after they show it.

- The rest of the students in the class will then list as many things as they can remember about the item.

- After the students are done writing down their responses, I ask the presenter to share with the class why they chose this item. After the student is done sharing, I ask the rest of the students to comment on what they wrote down. The result is that this one item ends up triggering many different memories from the past school years.

- After the discussion, I explain how the semantic network model works. I then tell the students that our long-term memory system is a web of associations. For example, the item shown triggered a dozen or so other memories.

- I also point out to the students that when they were smiling or laughing they brought up other funny things that happened. I then explain how this is an example of mood-congruent memories. When we are happy, we remember happy things.

Conclusion:

This activity usually takes two to three days to get through all the students. At the end of the presentations, I have the students type and organize what they wrote down for each school year. Over the years, students have expanded these requirements and turned this project into a personalized yearbook. They add pictures, awards, report cards, use nicer paper, and even get them bound. Students enjoy this activity as it makes them feel proud of what they have accomplished, while building confidence for facing future challenges.

Activity 40: Memory Exercise: Matching Cards

Contributed by Micah Owen
Ballard High School
Louisville, Kentucky

Mr. Owen is a seventh-year teacher at Ballard High School, where he teaches AP Psychology and the Honors Psychology classes. He has been an AP reader for two years and is looking forward to this year's grading, which will be in Louisville, Kentucky. He loves what he is teaching and the school where he is located. He has been married to his wife, Jennifer, for seven years. They have two dogs and no kids.

This activity is to be included with the Memory unit. It can be used before the topic of memory is discussed or after to illustrate various concepts of short-term memory. I have found that students are easily confused about the different memory systems and the properties of each. A simple game helps to show the limits of short-term memory, as well as ways to increase its duration and capacity.

Memory Exercise: Matching Cards

Have students get in pairs and give each pair a copy of certain pictures. I use clip art of simple drawings of things such as cars, hammers, keys, turtles, clocks, stars, and sharks. Have the students cut out two sets of each picture to make cards, turn the cards face down jumbled up, and instruct the students to play a classic memory game in which they must try to match picture cards. If a student makes a match, they get another turn; if they miss, they must flip both cards back over.

Some questions to consider asking either in a discussion or written form after the activity are:
1. What limits to your short-term memory did you experience?
2. What strategies did you use to help deal with the limits of your short-term memory?
3. What are the advantages and disadvantages to the ways in which our memory systems work?

Activity 41: Sleep Log

Contributed by Amy L. Malin
Stephen F. Austin High School
Sugar Land, Texas

Ms. Malin has had the pleasure of teaching Psychology and AP Psychology at Austin High School for 10 years, where she currently chairs the social studies department and sponsors her school's Psychology club. Ms. Malin wrote the district curriculum course outline for Psychology and AP Psychology for Fort Bend Independent School District and is a member of Teachers of Psychology in Secondary Schools and the Texas Council for Social Studies. In the summers, she enjoys teaching enrichment social studies courses and mentoring social studies student teachers at Rice University's Summer School for grades 8–12.

One thing I have noticed about our student body (and our faculty) is that they are not very sleep savvy. Most students undervalue the importance of sleep and do not recognize the relationship between the amount of sleep they obtain and their mood, thoughts, behavior, efficiency, and general health. To help students realize this connection, I have them chart their sleep, mood, and energy over a period of two weeks while we study consciousness. Students link their hours of sleep with dream recall, mood, energy, caffeine intake, and entrainment, all while demonstrating the utility of subjective reports. After the two weeks, students are given a chance to reflect upon and draw conclusions about their sleep habits.

Sleep Log

On the Monday before we begin studying consciousness, I give my students instructions for their sleep log. Each student is to create a chart using the following headings and then keep up with the chart to the best of his/her ability for two full weeks. These are the required headings:

1	2	3	4	5	6	7	8	9
Date/ Day	Time to Bed	Time Awake	Dreams? (include summary if yes)	No. of Hours Slept	How Did You Feel Upon Waking?	No. of Naps Today	Energy Level Throughout the Day	Caffeine Intake

Because the log is each student's subjective report, I allow the student to personalize it and complete it in ways that make sense to him/her. However, a key must be included so that I can decipher what is meant if only a number is provided in columns 6, 7, 8, or 9. Students can add more columns if they so desire. I have found students get confused by the column headings and when to fill them in, so I go through an example with them beforehand. For example, columns 1–2 would be filled out on Monday night, columns 3–6 would be filled out Tuesday morning, and columns 7–9 would be filled out Tuesday evening (all relating to Monday night's sleep).

After the two weeks are up and our unit on consciousness has ended, I have students complete these questions:

1. What was your average number of hours of sleep per night?

2. How many dreams did you recall during the two weeks? If you recalled fewer than eight dreams, what are some of the reasons why you may not have recalled your dreams? What could you do to change that? If you recalled eight or more, what explains your excellent recall abilities?

3. If you did record a dream, why do you think you had this dream (what might it mean)? Pick any dream out of the several you may have had.

4. Compare or contrast your sleep patterns during the week with your sleep patterns during the weekend. How did the differences (or similarities) in your sleep patterns affect your energy level and general attitude during those two parts of the week? Be sure to use two examples from your log to support your answer.

5. After all that you have learned about the sleep cycle and entrainment, do you feel like you physically and mentally get enough sleep to allow you to *fully* and *actively* participate in the events of your day? Explain. If you answered no, please continue with the following questions: What could you reasonably do to change your sleep habits to allow you to get the best/most sleep? What is stopping you from doing these things?

Activity 42: Hypnosis

Contributed by Tammy Dorgan
Larry A. Ryle High School
Union, Kentucky

Ms. Dorgan graduated from Northern Kentucky University in 2003 with a bachelor of arts degree in history and social studies. She has been teaching General Psychology and AP Psychology for three years at Ryle High School in Union, Kentucky. She is currently working on her master's degree in school counseling through Northern Kentucky University. She is a member of the American Psychological Association, Teachers of Psychology in Secondary Schools, National Council for the Social Studies, and Phi Alpha Theta. Ms. Dorgan was named to *Who's Who Among American High School Teachers* in 2006.

After discussing hypnosis as an altered state of consciousness with my students, I take a class period and hypnotize them. The hypnosis, including the discussion, often takes the full 55 minutes of the class. The hypnosis activity was introduced to me at a summer AP institute by Julie Caldwell. I have used this activity every year to demonstrate hypnosis. The students enjoy it, as well as the conversation that it fosters.

Hypnosis

Instructions:

1. Have students get comfortable in their desks or lying on the floor. Tell them to uncross their legs. Turn the lights off and close the blinds. You want as little stimulus as possible. I put a sign on the door that states, "Do Not Disturb." I also push the desks to each side of the room and allow the students to bring in blankets or something comfortable to lie on.

2. Start with the toes; tell your students to feel the muscles in their toes and then tell those muscles to relax. Then move to the arch of the foot and then slowly up the body to the back of the neck. Tell them to command the muscles to relax and give way to the stress of the day. Tell them it is all right if their muscles get tense before they relax. Speak softly and slowly. If they fall asleep, it is fine. It just means that they are really relaxed. When you get to the neck, start again with their fingers and work your way back to the neck. Go up the back of the head and then forward down the face. Name the scalp, eyes, cheeks, lips, and jaw. They are now relaxed.

3. Tell the students to picture in their heads a building that they are walking toward. Have them see all the details about the building and have them walk toward the front door. When they reach the front door, they should open it. As they open the front door, they find themselves in a lobby. Tell them to look around and find the elevator. Have them put a lot of detail into the lobby. Are there a lot of plants in the lobby? Are there people in the lobby? Do they hear music playing? Tell them to look for the elevator; they are to take the elevator down alone. As each floor goes by, they are relaxing more and more.

4. When the elevator stops, it opens onto a path in a meadow. Visualize it for them using all the senses (smell the honeysuckle, feel the warm sunlight streaming on your face, hear the birds chirping, etc.). The more detail, the better. Tell them that this is their safe place and they can go there anytime. Have them lie down in the meadow and watch the clouds in the sky. Visualize!

5. After a few minutes, have them stand up in the meadow and follow the path that leads to a forest. Inside the forest, there is a clearing and a cottage. Be very descriptive. Have them walk into the cottage. It is one room, and it is empty except for a table in the center with a piece of sculpture on it that is a gift for them. Tell them to examine the sculpture. Let them decide what it is. Each one will be different.

6. Walk them back through the woods, down the path, through the meadow, to the elevator. They get in the elevator and press the button to go up. Give them the command to feel relaxed, refreshed, peaceful, and strong. They wake up a little as each floor goes by, and when the elevator stops, they get off the elevator in the lobby and walk toward the front door. Give them the command that they will awake when they touch the handle to the front door. This may take a few minutes.

7. After everyone awakes, discuss with them what occurred, how they feel, what they remember, etc. Include in the discussion the sculptures. The sculptures are symbolic of something their mind is dealing with right now; for example, wings may symbolize leaving for college. Have the class guess at what the sculptures mean while still in the dark (they bond that way). Sometimes you will get statues of naked males and females, and sometimes they change. Give it your best guess.

8. The important thing to remember is to *never* take them back in time! This is dangerous because it could bring up repressed memories; you don't want to go there. Leave that for the licensed professional.

Alternate walk: Do steps 1–3 with the elevator adding years to their lives as it goes down until 10 years have passed. When the doors open, they will wake up in their beds 10 years from now and ready to go to work. Take them through a workday: breakfast (alone or with someone?), carpooling or driving alone, work space, phone calls, going home for lunch, and then walking into their house, which becomes the elevator. Years are taken off for each floor they go up until they are the right age. Make the details vague, and have them fill them in so that they can individualize their lives. Ask when they are awake about what they saw in the future for themselves. This is an exercise to try and get them to look at their goals for their lives.

Activity 43: Icekube: An Addiction Simulation

Contributed by Charlie Blair-Broeker
Cedar Falls High School (Iowa)
Cedar Falls, Iowa

Mr. Blair-Broeker has taught Psychology at Cedar Falls High School (Iowa) since 1978. He has been involved in a number of American Psychological Association (APA) initiatives, serving as a member of the task force that authored the "National Standards for High School Psychology," as chair of the executive board of Teachers of Psychology in Secondary Schools, and as co-editor of the fourth volume of the *APA Activities Handbook for the Teaching of Psychology*. For three years, Charlie co-directed Teaching the Science of Psychology, a summer institute for high school psychology teachers supported by the National Science Foundation and the Northern Kentucky University Foundation. He has been a rubric writer, table leader, or reader for AP psychology examinations since the test was first administered in 1992, completed a three-year term on the AP Psychology Test Development Committee, and is a psychology consultant for the College Board. Charlie has led dozens of teacher workshops across the United States and Canada. Among his teaching awards are the Grinnell College Outstanding Iowa Teacher Award, the University of Iowa Distinguished Teacher Award, and the APA Division 2 Teaching Excellence Award.

This simulation helps students understand the complex interaction of factors in a bio-psycho-social model of drug addiction.

Icekube: An Addiction Simulation

Materials:

Each student will need an "Icekube" student handout and a ball of twine (the cheaper and itchier, the better).

Method:

The general procedures for the simulation are described on the student handout. I run the simulation over two school days; for example, from the time a class meets on Monday until it meets again on Wednesday. Having the simulation on school days means student will not be able to simply stay at home for most of the experience.

I try to have students get parental permission at least a month before the simulation. This means parents have usually forgotten about the assignment by the time it rolls around.

I hold an "Icekube Anonymous" meeting during the class period when the simulation ends. Students arrange their desks in a circle. I step out in the hall, knock on the door, and wait for a student to answer. I enter and say, "Is this the Icekube Anonymous meeting? My name is Charlie, and I am a former 'kube user." The format becomes a springboard to discuss their experiences, what was surprising, how they felt, ways in which this experience might be similar to and dissimilar to actual addiction, suggestions for improving the activity, and so forth. It's usually a lively discussion.

The free write is due two days after the simulation ends.

Discussion:

This can be a powerful simulation. You need to be aware going in that this is an issue that will have touched the lives of some of your students. They may be dealing with drug problems of their own, and they may have family members or close friends who are struggling with addiction. It is a fun activity, but I treat the topic with seriousness and stress repeatedly that real addictions can produce tremendous suffering.

Participation in this activity should be strictly voluntary. Parental approval is essential at the high school level. In the few cases where parents have refused to allow their children to participate, it is usually because there is a family member who is struggling with a drug problem.

I stress in advance that some students are uncomfortable with the activity because it is usually necessary to lie to hide icekube use from family and friends.

References:

Campbell, T. C. (1999). Addiction simulation exercise: Ice cube addiction. In L. T. Benjamin, B. F. Nodine, R. M. Ernst, & C. T. Blair-Broeker (Eds.) *Activities handbook for the teaching of psychology* (Vol. 4). Washington, DC: American Psychological Association.

McNeece, C. A., & DiNitto, D. M. (1998). *Chemical dependency: A systems approach* (2nd ed.). Boston: Allyn & Bacon.

Icekube Student Handout

This is an exercise to help you experience and understand, through a safe, active-learning exercise, the complex interaction of biological, psychological, and sociological processes produced by drug addiction. It allows you to experience, firsthand, some of what happens to a person who is actually addicted to a drug.

This exercise is optional. Students who have done it recommend it highly, but if you or your parents prefer, there is an alternate assignment available. If you start the simulation, you may choose to stop participating at any time.

Guidelines:

1. The exercise will run for 48 consecutive hours.

2. Your "drug of choice" is icekube. You used to be able to "get off" on water alone, but now you need the frozen version. This is similar to making a progression from, for example, marijuana to hashish. In order to distinguish between regular ice cubes and your icekube, you must make the icekube from water that has been colored with a few drops of food coloring.

3. Thirst represents your physical craving for icekube. Every time you drink any liquid, you must have icekube in it. This will be difficult and require much planning. It includes drinking fountains, beverages from cans, hot drinks, and late night sips of water after you have awakened from a deep sleep. You do not need icekube with liquids generally consumed with a spoon (e.g., soup), the water you use to brush your teeth (as long as you limit the process to swishing and spitting), and medicines.

4. Consider icekube socially unacceptable and illegal. Do not let nonusers see you possessing or consuming the drug. This applies to family and friends. The only people with whom it is acceptable to be open about your use of icekube are other "addicts" who are participating in this exercise or "former users" who participated in previous semesters. Hiding your "stash" and your habit will take considerable effort.

5. To simulate the outward signs of addiction (needle tracks, weight loss, bloodshot eyes, etc.), you will be given a three-foot length of twine that must be kept next to your skin for the entire exercise. You may tie it around your arm, leg, or waist, but you should try your best to hide it from nonusers so they don't ask questions and put you in a difficult position. The twine will also serve as a constant physical reminder of your participation.

6. To simulate the obsessive quality of addiction, you are to keep an hourly log (during waking hours only) of your experience. Each hour you are to jot a very brief note to yourself about your experiences, feelings, or thoughts regarding the simulation. The note may be very brief. You may want to keep this log on a piece of paper that you fold up and carry in your pocket; there is no expectation that it will be well written. If you have a watch or cell phone with an hourly chime, set it to help you remember to make an entry each hour.

7. At the end of the simulation, write a two-page free write describing your reaction(s) to the experience. Write it in any manner you feel appropriate. The goal is to convince me you've put some thought into what happened. Please attach your log (in its original rough form) to your free write.

The more you involve yourself in the simulation, the more worthwhile it will be. Try to follow the guidelines to the very best of your ability. *However, please exercise good judgment in regard to potential problems that could be produced by this assignment.* For example, don't fill out your log entry in the middle of an exam for another teacher. Don't continue to lie to a friend who is getting angry about your strange behavior. Don't get dehydrated at cross-country practice because you have no water with icekube to drink. In a word, *think!*

Parent/Guardian Approval: I have read the assignment and approve of my son/daughter's participation.

_____

Activity 44: Psychoactive Drug Project

Contributed by David Meixl
Appleton North High School
Appleton, Wisconsin

Mr. Meixl was born and raised in the Appleton area. After completing a secondary education degree in Minnesota, he decided to move back to the Fox Cities. Mr. Meixl feels that Appleton is a great place to raise a family and teach high school. He taught for nine years at a parochial high school before teaching in the Appleton district. During his tenure, he has taught a wide variety of social studies courses. His favorite is psychology because it takes place all around us and is a practical and applicable course. The students find the subject material riveting and work hard to understand the concepts.

It is impossible to study all psychoactive drugs and their effects. This project allows students to choose a drug and create an oral presentation. I introduce the project after an initial lecture on drugs and how they affect our state of consciousness.

Psychoactive Drug Project

Psychoactive drugs are a part of our lives. Whether they are over the counter, prescription, illegal, or otherwise, they have an impact by helping or hindering our health and performance.

Directions:

Select a drug you want to research and report on. These will be assigned on a first-come, first-serve basis, so have a few drugs in mind when it comes time to choose.

Your report should include the following information:

1. Description of the drug, including its makeup (4 pts)
2. Classification of the drug (2 pts)
3. Slang terms or street names for the drug (2 pts)
4. Ways to ingest the drug (2 pts)
5. Similar drugs with the same effects (2 pts)
6. Medicinal use of the drug (2 pts)
7. Effects (5 pts)
   a. Psychological effects to the brain
   b. Physiological effects on the rest of the body
   c. Duration of effects (both short and long term)
8. Dependence (psychological and physical) (3 pts)
9. A visual aid (3 pts)
10. A fooler, which is a falsehood, or something that is definitely not true about your drug. Stay away from numbers.

Presentation:

- On the day of the presentation, the presenter(s) will hand an *outline* to the evaluator.
- You will be graded on the criteria above.
- You may work with another person.

This project will be due on _____ and is worth _____ points.

A list of drugs is located below. If there is one not listed that you would like to report on, check with me for approval.

Drug List:

Alcohol	Heroin	OxyContin
Amphetamines	Inhalants	Peyote
Barbiturates	Ketamine	Phenothiazines
Butyrophenones	LSD	Phencyclidine (PCP)
Caffeine	Marijuana	Psilocybin
Clozapine	Muscarine	(hallucinogenic mushrooms)
Cocaine	MDMA (ecstasy)	Rohypnol (date rape drug)
Codeine	Meprobamate	Secobarbital
Crack	Mescaline	Steroids
Crystal meth	Methadone	Strychnine
Datura	Methylphenidate	Thalidomide
Dextroamphetamine	Morphine	Theophylline
GHB	Nicotine	Tranquilizers
Hashish	Opium	

Activity 45: Cognition, Color, and Concept: Using Set, Observation, and Inquiry to Problem Solve

Contributed by Randy Ernst
Lincoln Public Schools
Lincoln, Nebraska

Mr. Ernst taught psychology at Lincoln High School, North Star High Schools, and Nebraska Wesleyan University. He is a co-author of the *National Standards for the Teaching of High School Psychology*, co-editor of the American Psychological Association's *Activities Handbook for the Teaching of Psychology (Vol. IV)*, and author of the College Board's *Teacher's Guide for Advanced Placement Psychology*. Randy has chaired the Teachers of Psychology in Secondary Schools (TOPSS) executive board, served on the College Board's AP Psychology Test Development Committee, and has been a table leader, question leader, and exam leader at the annual Advanced Placement Psychology Reading. He has authored or co-authored several TOPSS unit plans and has worked to infuse positive psychology across the K–12 curriculum. Mr. Ernst has provided in-service on the teaching of psychology to teachers around the United States and Canada and is an international psychology consultant for the College Board. Honors include Nebraska's 2006 Social Studies Educator of the Year Award, the National Association for the Advancement of Colored People's (Nebraska Chapter) 2004 Service to Children Award, and Time Warner's "Crystal Apple" National Teacher Award. Both the American Psychological Association and the University of Nebraska have recognized Mr. Ernst for excellence in teaching.

This demonstration shows that given the proper set, our visual senses can mislead us into making incorrect conclusions about stimuli received.

Cognition, Color, and Concept:
Using Set, Observation, and Inquiry to Problem Solve

Materials:

You'll need a color printout of the phrase "HIDE the COOKIE in the BOX," typed exactly as it appears in this sentence (without quotation marks). The capital letters need to be in red, the remaining letters in blue. You'll also need several 6-inch glass stir rods (students can share if you don't have a class set). Stir rods can be ordered online or borrowed from the chemistry teacher. Quarter-inch plastic tubing (4 inches in length) for each student is optional. Finally, a box of plastic baggies would come in handy.

Procedure:

Pair up the students in your class. Proceed with a discussion on the relationship between color and wavelength (this is the set). Note that red wavelengths are over 700 nanometers (billionths of a meter), while blue is much shorter at 500 nanometers. Ask students to generate how this affects what we see when we look at different colors, perhaps speculating on reasons the sky is blue instead of red without actually really providing any concrete answers.

Hand each pair of students a baggie containing the sheet of paper with "HIDE the COOKIE in the BOX" typed out, instructing students to take the paper out of the baggie and place it on a flat surface, face up. Generate some quick, accurate observations about what they see (i.e., six words, some words in red, some words in lowercase, etc.) and put these observations on the board.

Next, ask students to place the baggie over the paper and generate how this changes what they see. (They won't have much to say here.)

Hand out the glass stir rods. Instruct students to roll the rod over the words. Gather more observations (words are elongated, distorted, hard to read, etc.). Finally, ask students to lift the rod 1/4 inch off the paper above the words, asking them to read the words again. This time, they will observe that the blue words are upside down. Ask students to independently write down a hypothesis as to why the blue words are inverted. Collect and read some of the hypotheses to the class. A majority of the students will hypothesize wavelength as the reason for the inversion. All of these hypotheses are wrong, as *all* the words are upside down, due to the prism effect of the glass.

Discussion:

The red letters do not appear inverted because they are symmetrical. Unless the students are well grounded in their understanding of sensation and perception (how the eye inverts all images, as does a cylindrical glass object) or are able to break out of the wavelength set, they will not generate the correct hypothesis.

Writing Component:

Ask students to write an explanation of (A) possible reasons for the faulty hypotheses and (B) the tests or methods they would use to support or reject the hypothesis that wavelength was the reason for the inversion.

Activity 46: Fill in the Blanks

Contributed by Susan Johnson
Oswego High School
Oswego, Kansas

Ms. Johnson has taught Psychology at Oswego High School for the past 22 years and has been an adjunct instructor in Business and Psychology at Labette Community College for the past 26 years. Ms. Johnson received her bachelor's degree in education/business and her master's degree in counseling from Pittsburg State University. She is a National Board–certified counselor and is a member of Teachers of Psychology in Secondary Schools, Phi Kappa Phi, the American Counseling Association, and the Kansas Counseling Association. She received the Kansas School Counselor Association Outstanding School Counselor of the Year Award in 1998 and the Southeast Kansas Counseling Association Outstanding Counselor of the Year Award in 1996.

The following examples can be used during discussions on language, intelligence, problem solving, or the brain. The students will have trouble with the first example and probably get a little angry, but the second example will be much easier to understand. If you have the consonants, you can read anything. But if you only have the vowels, it is very hard to read. So, if you have trouble reading a word, block out the vowels. Your brain will be able to fill in the blanks.

Fill in the Blanks

_ _e _o_o_ _e_

 _e_ i_ a _ou_a_ _o_o_ i_ _u_a_ _u__ue. I_ _a_ ___ _o_i_e
_o_e, _o_e_, _a__e_, _o_a___, o_ a_ e_e__e___. I_ i_ a _o_o_
_o_ ___i__a_ a__ _a_e__ie'_ _a_. I_ _a_ _e a "_e_ _e__e_ _a_"
o_ _ou _a_ "_e i_ __e _e_." _ea_i__ _e_ _a_ _oo__ _ou_
_o__i_e__e.

After giving your students a few minutes to complete the one above, give them this one on a separate sheet.

Th_ C_l_r R_d

 R_d _s _ p_p_l_r c_l_r _n h_m_n c_lt_r_. _t c_n symb_l_z_ l_v_,
p_w_r, d_ng_r, r_y_lty, _r _n _m_rg_ncy. _t _s _ c_l_r f_r Chr_stm_s
_nd V_l_nt_n_'s D_y. _t c_n b_ _ "r_d l_tt_r d_y" _r y__ c_n "b_
_n th_ r_d." W__r_ng r_d c_n b__st y__r c_nf_d_nc_.

Answer Key:

The Color Red

 Red is a popular color in human culture. It can symbolize love, power, danger, royalty, or an emergency. It is a color for Christmas and Valentine's Day. It can be a "red letter day" or you can "be in the red." Wearing red can boost your confidence.

Activity 47: Intelligence

Contributed by Tammy Dorgan
Larry A. Ryle High School
Union, Kentucky

Ms. Dorgan graduated from Northern Kentucky University in 2003 with a bachelor of arts degree in history and social studies. She has been teaching General Psychology and AP Psychology for three years at Ryle High School in Union, Kentucky. She is currently working on her master's degree in school counseling through Northern Kentucky University. She is a member of the American Psychological Association, Teachers of Psychology in Secondary Schools, National Council for the Social Studies, and Phi Alpha Theta. Ms. Dorgan was named to *Who's Who Among American High School Teachers* in 2006.

For the Intelligence unit, I have students take a small sample of a variety of intelligence tests and then compare the tests. This fosters discussion about bias and the debates about intelligence tests and scores. I give them a sample test by printing out tests from the Web sites listed in the activity or taking them from books with IQ tests.

Intelligence

The 10-item *Australian/American Intelligence Test* is drawn from typical items on standard Western-European intelligence tests. Go to http://wilderdom.com/personality/intelligenceAustralianAmericanTest.html.

The 10-item *Original Australian Intelligence Test* is based on the culture of the Edward River Australian Aboriginal community in North Queensland. Go to http://wilderdom.com/personality/intelligenceOriginalAustralian.html.

One facetious attempt to develop an intelligence test that utilizes distinctively black-ghetto experiences is the *Chitling Test*. It is a humorous example that demonstrates well the built-in cultural bias found in most IQ tests. The Chitling Test (formally, the Dove Counterbalance General Intelligence Test) was designed by Adrian Dove, a black sociologist. Aware of the dialect differences between different ethnic and socioeconomic groups, he developed this exam as a half-serious attempt to show that American children are not all speaking the same language. Those students who are not "culturally deprived" will score well. The original test has 30 multiple-choice questions. Go to http://wilderdom.com/personality/intelligenceChitlingTestShort.html.

Among the many sample tests I include is the Mensa workout. I usually give students the Mensa workout first, then proceed with the other tests, ending with the Chitling test.

The Web sites above are easy to access, and you are allowed to print out the tests. I have found that, after doing this activity, the students have a great discussion about the role of intelligence tests and the biases associated with them.

Activity 48: Suicide Discussion

Contributed by Rob Nelson
Shorewood High School
Shorewood, Washington

Dr. Nelson's life experiences have included teaching World Geography and Social Psychology for the Shoreline School District in the state of Washington for the past 30 years. Dr. Nelson has traveled in Europe, Africa, Central America, Micronesia, and Asia. He lived overseas for the better part of 20 years and completed high school at the American Academy in Athens, Greece. He also served four years in the U.S. Navy with two tours in Vietnam. Dr. Nelson has studied post-secondary education and received his master's and doctorate degrees in adult education and the Running Start program.

Learning Objectives:

1. To make students aware of the problem of suicide in our society

2. To examine historical and cultural attitudes toward suicide

3. To explore some major theories about the causes of suicide

4. To discuss specific problems and pressures that often contribute to suicidal feelings

5. To correct commonly held misconceptions about suicide

6. To describe common warning signs of suicide

7. To explain what steps may be taken to help a suicidal person

Suicide Discussion

Of all forms of death, suicide has long been among the most feared and misunderstood. Self-destruction is generally viewed as abhorrent and insane; yet most of us have thought about it at one time or another. However fleetingly the notion of suicide may cross our minds, and however quickly we dismiss it, the idea and the possibility are there. Each of us has the power to end our own life. It may be in part because this power is so frightening that suicide is considered to be a taboo subject.

Historically, in Western culture, the act of killing oneself has been regarded as shameful, mad, even wicked. The Catholic Church has deemed suicide a sin; some laws have classified it as a crime. Popularly, suicide has often been viewed as a sign of weakness, of inability to face life, to deal with problems, to take responsibility, to stand up to hardship. Those who commit or attempt suicide have been regarded as somehow inferior, and the stigma attached to them has often been extended to their families as well.

Today, we are beginning to look at suicide in a more enlightened way. We have become more open to discussing suicide, and accordingly, the subject has become somewhat less threatening. Progress has been made in understanding the causes, identifying potential suicides, and helping those who are in danger of killing themselves.

About half a million Americans attempt suicide each year; approximately 35,000 succeed. Although the suicide rate may vary among various groups, suicide is a problem common to all people, regardless of age, race, class, or sex.

Statistics can answer the question of who commits suicide, but the question of why people kill themselves is more difficult. Emile Durkheim, a nineteenth-century French sociologist, considered social factors most important. Sigmund Freud held that suicide was related to death-oriented, aggressive instincts that all humans share. More recently, Karl Menninger, a psychiatrist, has explored different ways in which suicidal tendencies are expressed, for example, taking extreme risks or drinking heavily over a long period of time.

A person under severe stress may commit suicide. Deep depression is often linked with suicide, and depression may be caused by a number of things. Hopelessness, for example, is thought to be a leading factor in suicidal depression among young urban blacks. Among all young people, loneliness, isolation, or the loss of a loved one are often linked with suicide.

What is the difference between those who commit suicide and others who experience similar problems without killing themselves? The difference seems to be in the intensity of the feelings experienced. A suicidal person becomes so overwhelmed by his or her feelings that he or she loses sense of perspective and cannot entertain the possibility that things can get better.

We must recognize the problem of suicide, learn more about it, and take action to help people who may want to kill themselves. We must overcome our ignorance of suicide to prevent it. One common myth is that only a certain type of person commits suicide—that a person has to be "crazy" to commit suicide and that "nice" people don't do it.

Most suicides could be prevented if people would discard myths and misconceptions and learn to recognize the clues, or warning signals, that a suicidal person often gives about his or her intentions. One important warning signal is an actual statement of suicidal intentions. It is a common misconception that people who talk about committing suicide never do it; most people who commit suicide do talk about it beforehand.

Some other warning signals are less direct. A person might seem preoccupied with death or remark that others would be better off if she or he were dead. Sometimes we might guess a person's suicidal intentions because of certain preparations the person makes, such as putting business affairs in order or giving away prized possessions. Severe depression is another danger signal, as deeply depressed people are more likely to become suicidal. Changes in a person's behavior can indicate serious depression; for instance, loss of interest in activities, social withdrawal, loss of appetite, excessive sleepiness, or insomnia.

It is important to remember that while severe depression may bring on suicidal feelings, the danger of suicide is not over as soon as the depression begins to lift. While in a depressed state, the person may have lacked the energy to act on his or her thoughts, but when the depression begins to abate, the person may regain enough energy to attempt to suicide. The watchfulness of friends and relatives should continue both during and several months after a period of depression.

(continued)

An actual suicide attempt is another warning signal. An attempt may be a "cry for help;" yet, people often dismiss an unsuccessful suicide attempt as merely a dramatic gesture. Unfortunately, if a person who attempts suicide does not get the help that she or he needs, the person may try again and eventually succeed in committing suicide.

What can we do? We can first talk to the person to try to dispel feelings of loneliness and isolation. Second, we must find professional help. Suicide prevention centers, mental health clinics and hospitals, doctors, clergy, and teachers are several sources of assistance. A professional's help is needed to get the individual past the crisis.

Once a person has gotten past the immediate crisis of suicide, he or she will probably still need to deal with the problems that caused the person to consider suicide. But these problems are not insurmountable. Severe depression may be medically treated, and psychiatric counseling can be effective in helping people identify and deal with their problems.

A person in the midst of a suicidal crisis may be without hope, but once the crisis is past, the world may offer hope once more. By identifying and helping a suicidal person, we are not only preventing death; we are preserving the possibility of a fulfilling and productive life.

Discussion Questions:

1. What is one possible explanation for the great increase in suicides among young urban blacks? Answer: Blacks now have higher hopes and expectations, but they are still frustrated by limited opportunities and suffer from feelings of hopelessness and despair.

2. What most often triggers suicide among young people? Answer: Feelings of isolation and loneliness often drive young people to commit suicide.

3. What is the main difference between a suicidal and a nonsuicidal person facing similar problems? Answer: A suicidal person has lost her or his sense of perspective and can't recognize that things may well get better.

4. Are most suicidal individuals completely committed to killing themselves? Answer: No; most suicidal people do not truly want to die and hope they may be saved.

5. Is there such a thing as a suicide type? Answer: No; any person may become suicidal, and often a suicidal person appears to be no different from anyone else.

6. Why are stereotypes of suicidal individuals dangerous? Answer: People often ignore suicide warnings because the person doesn't fit their stereotype of the "suicide type."

7. How should a statement such as, "One of these days I'm going to kill myself," be regarded? Answer: Such a statement should always be taken seriously as a possible warning signal of suicide.

8. What types of statements are indirect suicide warning signals? Answer: A person might seem preoccupied with death, or the person might make oblique references to dying, such as, "You'd all be better off without me."

9. What arrangements might a person make which could warn you that he or she is contemplating suicide? Answer: Someone might put his or her financial affairs in order or give away prized possessions.

10. What are some symptoms of severe depression? Answer: Loss of interest in activities that were formerly enjoyed, withdrawal from social contact, loss of appetite, and excessive sleepiness or wakefulness

11. Why is the danger of suicide not over when severe depression begins to subside? Answer: A deeply depressed person often does not have the energy to act on her or his suicidal thoughts, but when the depression begins to lift, some of her or his energy returns, and the person may become capable of carrying out her or his intention.

12. What should friends and family of a suicidally depressed person do during the period when the depression begins to lift? Answer: They should continue to be alert and prepared to help because the danger of suicide is not over.

13. Why is a suicide attempt often called a "cry for help"? Answer: By attempting suicide, an individual is often trying to communicate desperation to others and warn them that he or she needs help.

(continued)

14. Why are "cries for help" often unheeded? Answer: People refuse to take the person seriously, thinking that the person is merely trying to be dramatic and get attention.

15. How can talking to a suicidal person about her or his feelings help? Answer: Talking to the person may make her or him feel that someone cares and may penetrate the loneliness and isolation that a suicidal person often feels.

16. Why is it not advisable to act shocked or to speak moralistically to a suicidal person? Answer: This may deepen the person's sense of guilt and feelings of worthlessness.

17. What are some sources of professional help in dealing with a suicidal person? Answer: Suicide prevention centers, mental health clinics and hospitals, doctors, clergy, and teachers

18. What long-term help is available for someone past a suicidal crisis? Answer: Depression can sometimes be treated medically, and psychological counseling can be effective in helping people deal with their problems.

19. Is a suicidal person doomed to an unhappy existence for the rest of his or her life? Answer: No; once a suicidal crisis has passed, a person can lead a fulfilling life.

Activity 49: Psychological Disorders (Cooperative Group Project)

Contributed by Patricia Baima
Wheeling High School
Wheeling, Illinois

Ms. Baima currently teaches AP Psychology, Psychology I, and Psychology II at Wheeling High School. She has been employed by the school district for eight years. She is in the process of completing her master of arts in industrial/organizational psychology from Roosevelt University. She holds a master of arts in teaching from Aurora University and a bachelor of arts in psychology from Bradley University, graduating summa cum laude. She is a member of the following professional organizations: American Psychological Association, Teachers of Psychology Division, Society for Industrial and Organizational Psychology, National Council for the Social Studies, Phi Kappa Phi, and Psi Chi. She co-authored a journal article in *Early Childhood Research Quarterly*.

This project can be used when covering abnormal psychology. Each student receives directions and a rubric. Students are divided into groups of three, four, or five. Each group chooses one classification of disorders, researches the disorders, and then presents its information to the class. I usually have the following groups: anxiety disorders, mood disorders, personality disorders, dissociative disorders, somatoform disorders, and schizophrenic disorders. When the groups present, they must have a handout/quiz and brochure for each student in class. (I will collect the handout/quiz and brochure ahead of time and make copies for everyone.)

When students are graded on the rubric, each student in the group receives an individual grade as much as is possible. For example, each student earns five participation points each research day. If a student in one group is not doing research on a certain day, he/she will not earn five points for that day.

The rubric covers all the components of the overall grade. I have one rubric for each student, not one rubric per group. This allows individualized grading.

Psychological Disorders
(Cooperative Group Project)

Directions:

You will learn about different psychological disorders from your classmates. For five days, we will work on this project. As the semester progresses, we will spend approximately one week on each of the categories of disorders. You will present your information during the week we are discussing the unit that contains your disorder. You will have 30 to 40 minutes to present all of your information.

Day 1: The Introduction

1. You will receive the rubric for this assignment.

2. You will be divided into groups of three, four, or five students.

3. Your goal will be to design an informal presentation about your disorder. During your presentation, you will describe the disorder, explain the causes and treatment options according to the different psychological perspectives, describe the most popular treatment options today, and describe any "new" breakthroughs. Also, what may happen in the future with your disorder?

4. You will need to read about your disorder in your textbook. This can be one of your reference sources!

5. Begin to brainstorm on what your group would like to do for the classroom presentation. You can conduct a classroom lecture, a television news program (like *20/20*), a television talk show (like *Oprah*), or anything else that educates your fellow classmates on your disorder. You can use the chalkboard, the overhead, a PowerPoint demonstration, or a video clip with your presentation.

6. The following are the things that will need to be accomplished:

   A. A reference page with at least five sources listed. You can use your textbook for one of the sources, and the other four can be books, magazines, journal articles, CD-ROMs, or Internet sites that deal with your disorder. At least two sources must be from a book. (Your textbook will count as one of the two books!) Use APA style for your reference page.

   B. A poster that summarizes and describes your disorder.

   C. The classroom presentation needs to be between 30 and 40 minutes long. All information presented must be accurate. You will define the disorder, tell the causes of the disorder according to *all* of the perspectives, and tell the treatments for the disorder according to *all* of the perspectives. Then you can describe the most widely accepted perspective for explaining the cause and treatment of the disorder.

   D. All group members must participate in the classroom presentation, and all group members must show a thorough understanding of the disorder.

   E. Your group must be organized, and the presentation should be easy to follow.

   F. Your group will design a brochure for your disorder. This brochure needs to summarize basic facts about the disorder and the most widely accepted causes and treatments.

   G. Finally, your group will need to provide the class with a worksheet, handout, or quiz of the material you covered. A handout/quiz combination is also OK. Please try to make any worksheet/quiz rather short so that it does not take time away from your presentation.

   H. The following will be due on Day 5: a short outline of your presentation, your reference page, a sheet of paper explaining what everyone has done to help with this project, and your handout or anything else you will need to have copied. Everything else will be due the day of your presentation.

Days 2–4: Library Work

We will spend the entire hour in the library. You will find your five sources for your project, begin organizing your presentation, and begin fulfilling the "Day 5" requirements.

(continued)

Day 5: Finishing Up

You will have the entire hour to work on your group projects today. Due by the end of the period:

1. a short outline of your presentation
2. your reference page
3. a sheet of paper explaining what everyone has done to help with this project
4. your handout or anything else you will need to have copied (Everything else will be due the day of your presentation.)

Late work will not be accepted!

(continued)

Psychological Disorders
(Cooperative Group Project)

Rubric

Name _____   Hour _____

Disorder _____

Participation:

Day 1 (5) _____   Day 2 (5) _____

Day 3 (5) _____   Day 4 (5) _____

Day 5 (5) _____   Total _____(25)

Research and Other Work:

Reference page with at least five sources (and
    you actually used all of your sources)   (20) _____

Handout/Quiz   (20) _____

Brochure   (40) _____

Poster   (20) _____

                                                    Total _____ (100)

Classroom Presentation:

Accurately covered all of the necessary information:

    Definition of the disorder   (20) _____

    Causes of the disorder (all perspectives)   (20) _____

    Treatments for the disorder (all perspectives)   (20) _____

    The most popular treatment options and
        new breakthroughs   (20) _____

                                                    Total _____(80)

Explained difficult concepts simply so that everyone
    could understand the information   (20) _____

Well organized, easy to follow   (20) _____

Time = 30–40 min.   (10) _____

Everyone worked equally in your group   (15) _____

Demonstrated a thorough understanding of your disorder (individual grade)   (30) _____

                                                  Total _____ (95)

The above points will include the appearance of all material.

Please check all of your work for neatness, completeness, and mechanics.

Points may be adjusted for each group member depending on the circumstances.
    (Everyone in the group may *not* receive the same grade, if necessary!)

Your score _____ / 300 = _____% and a letter grade _____

Activity 50: **Psychological Movie Review**

Contributed by Joseph Geiger
Carl Sandburg High School
Orland Park, Illinois

Mr. Geiger received his bachelor of arts degree in psychology from Lewis University and his master of arts from Benedictine University. Presently, he is a tri-chairperson for the National Council for Social Studies (NCSS) Psychology Community and has presented at the NCSS conference for the past several years. Furthermore, he is a member of Teachers of Psychology in Secondary Schools, which is affiliated with the American Psychological Association. He has been teaching at Sandburg since 1995.

Students often become interested in the field of psychology to learn why people do the things they do and how they can correct other people's—as well as their own—problems. However, good ethics does not allow a person to go around and analyze and correct "issues" that people may have; thus, why not "kill two birds with one stone" by having students do something they enjoy at the same time they are doing something educational. This assignment does that.

The purpose of the "Psychological Movie Review" is to have students watch a popular film that contains a character that exhibits a psychological disorder and/or altered mental state discussed in the Abnormal Psychology unit. Then the students are to apply the *Diagnostic and Statistical Manual of Mental Disorders* (DSM) to explain, medically, how this subject fits the characteristics of a diagnosis.

Psychological Movie Review

Films often contain characters that exhibit psychological disorders and/or altered mental states. Your assignment is to:

- Watch a popular film that depicts a character with some form of psychological disorder covered in this course.

- Analyze how the content of the movie relates to course material on psychological disorders (see specific questions below).

- Splice four scenes, or write the tracking number from the start to the end of the scene, that back up the diagnosis. (Note: You are not being graded on how well you splice them together. Thus, if you use a home burner or recorder, you will not be down graded. However, if the video is poor quality, you will lose points. Ask me for clarification on this.)

- Present your video and diagnosis to the class in a 5- to 10-minute presentation. (You must show one scene [example] from your movie during your presentation.)

Your report must be:

- Typeset in Times or Times New Roman 12-point font

- 1-inch margins all around

- Turned in as a hard copy on the due date, as well as e-mailed or saved to a disk to hand in

After viewing your movie, answer the following questions:

1. What mental/psychological disorder is portrayed in the movie?

2. How does the movie relate to the course material we have covered in class or in your textbook? Please discuss *at least four specific scenes* and clarify how the movie and course material are related. This should be the main part of your report. You may point out how the movie illustrated course material and/or how it was not in accordance with what you have learned in this class.

3. Provide the full details of your diagnosis of the character, including the signs and symptoms apparent in the film, and relate them to the criteria for the disorder in the DSM-IV. This is similar to the previous question, but this is focusing on using the DSM-IV rather than course material.

4. Discuss the best forms of treatment for this person and the prognosis.

5. Discuss how the person would be characterized on each of the DSM-IV axes.

6. How has watching the movie contributed to your understanding of psychological disorders and their treatment? I don't have to agree with your opinions, but you are graded on showing an understanding of course material and the issues involved. (This is to be completed individually but still is to be typed on the template.)

Important Disclaimer:

These are not necessarily good movies, and please use discretion in selecting something that will not be offensive to you. Please be aware that some movies contain some violence and strong language. Each movie does deal with some aspect of a psychological disorder that we have discussed or will discuss in class, and the point of the assignment is for you to recognize and relate what you see in the movie to what you have learned or will learn about disorders and their treatment in the course. It's my way of helping you get ready for the final, including an excuse to watch a movie and say that you are "studying."

(continued)

The following is a list of videos that demonstrate psychological disorders and/or the characterization of a mental-health worker or facility.

12 Monkeys
A Beautiful Mind
Accidental Tourist
Affliction
An Angel at My Table
Analyze This
Antwone Fisher
Apocalypse Now
The Apostle
As Good As It Gets
At Close Range
Awakenings
Basketball Diaries
The Bell Jar
Benny and Joon
Bill
Birdy
Blackout
Boys Don't Cry
Captain Newman, MD
A Caveman's Valentine
Charly
Chasing Holden
Clean and Sober
Clockwork Orange
Coming Home
Copycat
Couch Trip
Cracker Factory
The Deer Hunter
Dominick and Eugene
Don Juan Demarco
Don't Say a Word
Dream Team
Drugstore Cowboy
Far From Heaven
Fatal Attraction
Fearless
Fight Club
Fisher King
Folks
Frances
Girl, Interrupted
Good Will Hunting
The Horse Whisperer
The Hours
I Am Sam
Identity
I Never Promised You a Rose Garden
In the Company of Men
I, Robot

Jacknife
Jacob's Ladder
Leaving Las Vegas
Life as a House
Lorenzo's Oil
The Man Who Wasn't There
Marnie
Mercury Rising
Misery
Mommie Dearest
Mr. Jones
My Sweet Killer
The Odd Couple
One Flew Over the Cuckoo's Nest
On Golden Pond
Ordinary Primal Fear
The Other Sister
Patch Adams
Postcards from the Edge
Prince of Tides
Radio
Radio Flyer
Rain Man
Raising Cain
Regarding Henry
Requiem for a Dream
Return of the Soldier
Road to Galveston
The Royal Tenenbaums
Rush
Safe
Secret Window
Seven
Shine
The Silence of the Lambs
Silent Fall
The Sixth Sense
Sling Blade
Snake Pit
Spellbound
Sybil
The Talented Mr. Ripley
Three Faces of Eve
Vertigo
What About Bob?
What Dreams May Come?
What's Eating Gilbert Grape?
When a Man Loves a Woman
White Oleander
Who's Afraid of Virginia Woolf?

(continued)

Student name: _____

Psychological disorder: _____

Name of movie: _____ Movie rating: _____

Character's name: _____ Actor's/actress's name: _____

How does the movie relate to the *course material* we have covered in class or in your textbook?

1. Scene 1 example
   - Tracking number beginning:
   - Tracking number ending:
   - Explanation of example:
2. Scene 2 example
   - Tracking number beginning:
   - Tracking number ending:
   - Explanation of example:
3. Scene 3 example
   - Tracking number beginning:
   - Tracking number ending:
   - Explanation of example:
4. Scene 4 example
   - Tracking number beginning:
   - Tracking number ending:
   - Explanation of example:

DSM-IV explanation

Characteristics of DSM-IV axis:
- Axis I identifies mental disorders.
- Axis II identifies personality disorders and mental retardation.
- Axis III identifies relevant physical diseases and conditions.
- Axis IV identifies the individual's psychosocial and environmental issues.
- Axis V is used by the clinician to assess an individual's overall functioning based on the 100-point scale called the global assessment of functioning (GAF).

   Viewer 1's thoughts of this disorder and psychological disorders

   Viewer 2's thoughts of this disorder and psychological disorders

Activity 51: Analysis of Arthur Miller's *All My Sons*

Contributed by Susan J. Phelon, M.Ed.
Ludlow High School
Ludlow, Massachusetts

Ms. Phelon has a bachelor of arts degree in psychology, a postgraduate teaching certification, and a master's degree in secondary education—all from Westfield State College in Westfield, Massachusetts. Working in a high school setting is a second career for her as she started teaching adult learners in the parent education department at Baystate Medical Center in Springfield, Massachusetts, 20 years ago. Before that, she was a stay-at-home mom (probably the most important position she has ever held). Ms. Phelon has been at Ludlow High School (her alma mater) for the past 10 years teaching Psychology I, Psychology II, Sociology, and U.S. History.

Arthur Miller's play *All My Sons* provides students with an opportunity to make connections between the characters and the psychological concepts that they have been studying. Defense mechanisms, psychological disorders, and society's influence on behavior are all aptly portrayed in the play. Students are expected to write their analyses based on the attached statements and questions.

Analysis of Arthur Miller's *All My Sons*

Content:

Produce a written analysis of Arthur Miller's play *All My Sons*.

Skills:

Correctly analyze the personalities of the characters.

Discuss society's influence on the characters' behavior.

Concepts:

Show an understanding of:

— Freud's defense mechanisms

— Psychological disorders

— Influence of society on behavior

Procedures:

Students are given the reading and the questions about a month prior to the due date. The teacher is available to answer any questions. Students are allowed to discuss the play, on their own time, if they would like, but the analysis must be their own. The students must hand in their analyses on the due date.

Interdisciplinary Connections:

This lesson connects well with the English department. Some students have read the play in their literature classes or are familiar with the author. This assignment allows the students to analyze the play on a different level than they would in their English class.

Analysis:

Using the following information to help you focus your thoughts, write a comprehensive essay that analyzes the play *All My Sons* from a psychological point of view. Discussions of the characters' use of defense mechanisms, psychological disorders, and the influence of society on individual behavior should be included.

1. The following two statements represent points of view. Include in your essay a discussion of the meaning of each point of view using examples from the play.
    A. Analysis of *All My Sons* makes clear that Miller is a "psychological" playwright. At his best, Miller has created clinical psychiatric case studies rather than mere sociological reports.
    B. The conflict between father and son in *All My Sons* is basically a conflict between two social attitudes.
2. Analyze the personalities of two major characters of your choice. Strengthen your generalizations with specific details and evidence.
3. In your essay, answer the following questions:
    A. Discuss the role of the women in the play. Did they "allow" the tragedy to occur?
    B. Who knew the truth? When? Analyze.
    C. Did the conclusion surprise you? Why or why not? Analyze.

Activity 52: Approaches to Therapy

Contributed by Cynthia Silovich
Fargo South High School
Fargo, North Dakota

This is **Ms. Silovich**'s 33rd year teaching Social Studies and English at Fargo South High School in Fargo, North Dakota. She has been teaching AP Psychology since 1993. She also works as an AP reader for psychology each summer.

This is a cooperative learning (jigsaw) assignment I use each year after the unit on abnormal psychology and as we are beginning the unit on therapy. I begin by presenting a case study of a person with depression. I sometimes use characters from books or case studies I find in other activities, or I show a video clip of someone with depression.

Approaches to Therapy

There will be six groups of four people each:

Group 1—Psychoanalytic/Psychodynamic

Group 2—Humanistic (Human Potential Movement)

Group 3—Behaviorist

Group 4—Biomedical (Biological)

Group 5—Cognitive

Group 6—Group Therapy

Assignment: Person 1

1. What background information do you need before deciding on treatment?
2. Would you involve family members, employers, clergy, friends, doctors, and other individuals in seeking information?
3. What are your therapeutic goals?
4. How does your approach view depression?

Assignment: Person 2

Using your textbook, describe the approach and find treatment possibilities.

Assignment: Person 3

Using the Internet, describe the approach and find treatment possibilities.

Assignment: Person 4

Using hard-copy references, describe the approach and find treatment possibilities.

Small-Group Work

After everyone in the four-person group has their information, they should share with the rest of the group. Each person in the group will need to make note of everyone's contribution. Then, as a group, suggest which treatment would be best for this client. Be sure you have a good understanding of the approach and therapy. You will be teaching others.

Large-Group Work

In this part of the assignment, you will be put in groups of six people, with one person from each of the six approaches. You will share the information you have on your approach with your group. Each person in this group will need to take notes on the shared information.

1. Describe the approach.
2. What background information is needed?
3. What are the therapeutic goals?
4. How does your approach view depression?
5. What are the treatment possibilities?
6. Which treatment was suggested?

Then, as a group, decide which approach or approaches would be most beneficial for the client. Which treatment would be best? Defend your answers.

You will be turning in your individual work, the small-group work for each approach, and the work done in the larger group.

(The students usually decide on a combination of treatments.)

Activity 53: Out of the Social Norm

Contributed by Marleine Kowal
Mahwah High School
Mahwah, New Jersey

Ms. Kowal lives in New Jersey with her husband and two sons. She received her bachelor of arts degree in history, psychology, and sociology from Thomas Edison State College, New Jersey, and received her master of arts degree in curriculum and instruction from The University of Missouri, Columbia. She has been teaching for nine years, the past seven at Mahwah High School in Mahwah, New Jersey. Before becoming a teacher, she was a restaurant manager for 10 years and then worked as an alcohol and drug counselor for two years. Ms. Kowal became a teacher because she wanted to share her love of history and psychology with young people.

After I teach my class about the Stanley Milgram experiment and the Stanford prison experiment, I assign a project to help my students understand the power of conformity in our society.

Out of the Social Norm

You are being asked to come to school or go to a public place (such as the mall) and experience what it is like to dress or behave against the social norm. As human beings, we tend to want to conform to those around us. You must either wear something that is against the school social norm or your own norm. *You may not wear or do anything that could offend anyone, dress out of dress code, or disrupt a teacher's class.* I trust you to use good judgment. If you are unsure whether your idea is appropriate, please ask. If you are going to a public place, you must go with someone else. Do not go door to door! The rest of the faculty has been informed of the experiment. Do not tell your classmates what you are doing. That would negate your results.

As you go through the day, you are to record other people's reactions to you and your feelings about those reactions. Be as detailed as possible. You will be required to hand in a typed copy detailing your experiment. It should include the following:

1. What was your experiment?
2. When did it take place?
3. Where did it take place?
4. What were your observations?
5. You should write a conclusion that explains what you learned from this experiment. How did it make you feel?
6. Why do you think it is important to us to conform?
7. Do you believe that there are times when a person should question the urge to conform?
8. After taking part in this exercise, do you think you will look differently at people who do not seem to conform to society? Please explain.

Ideas from past years:

— Stand up next to your desk to answer a question in class.
— Refer to your teachers as "ma'am" and "sir."
— Come to school in a wheelchair.
— Dress "punk" and shop in a "preppy" store, or dress "preppy" and shop in a "punk" store.

Activity 54: What Is Aggression?

Contributed by Charlie Blair-Broeker
Cedar Falls High School (Iowa)
Cedar Falls, Iowa

Mr. Blair-Broeker has taught Psychology at Cedar Falls High School (Iowa) since 1978. He has been involved in a number of American Psychological Association (APA) initiatives, serving as a member of the task force that authored the *National Standards for High School Psychology*, as chair of the executive board of Teachers of Psychology in Secondary Schools, and as co-editor of the fourth volume of the *APA Activities Handbook for the Teaching of Psychology*. For three years, Charlie co-directed Teaching the Science of Psychology, a summer institute for high school psychology teachers supported by the National Science Foundation and the Northern Kentucky University Foundation. He has been a rubric writer, table leader, or reader for AP psychology examinations since the test was first administered in 1992, completed a three-year term on the AP Psychology Test Development Committee, and is a psychology consultant for the College Board. Charlie has led dozens of teacher workshops across the United States and Canada. Among his teaching awards are the Grinnell College Outstanding Iowa Teacher Award, the University of Iowa Distinguished Teacher Award, and the APA Division 2 Teaching Excellence Award.

This activity illustrates that we often assume that a concept is well understood when, in fact, it's not. It demonstrates the importance of definitions and shows that psychologists do not agree on the definition of aggression. I use this activity before talking about factors that influence aggression.

What Is Aggression?

Materials:

Each student needs a copy of the aggression questionnaire and something to write with.

Procedure:

Pass out copies of the aggression questionnaire to the class and allow a few minutes for students to read through and check any statement believed to represent aggression. Students should not put their names on the papers.

Collect the papers and randomly redistribute them to the class. You can quickly determine how many students checked each item by asking for a show of hands, and then you can record the information on the board. Emphasize that students should raise their hands to indicate that the item was checked on the redistributed questionnaire—this way they are reporting anonymously on some other student's information and not divulging their own opinion publicly.

This information will provide the springboard for a very interesting discussion concerning the nature of aggression. I usually start by identifying items where the class is pretty evenly split and seeing where the discussion goes from there. Ludy Benjamin, the developer of the questionnaire, intentionally included items to represent issues related to aggression. These include:

- Living versus nonliving targets (items 9 and 23)
- Accident versus intention (items 8 and 21)
- Actual damage versus no physical damage (items 10, 13, and 18)
- Self-defense (items 3, 13, and 14)
- Duty or job responsibility (items 3, 4, 19, 20, and 22)
- Predation and instinctual behavior (items 1, 2, and 25)
- Survival (items 1, 6, and 16)
- Acts involving animals (items 7, 16, 17, 18, and 25)
- Mental acts (items 11 and 14)
- Inaction (items 12 and 15)
- Self-injury (item 24)
- Killing for sport (items 17 and 25)

It's helpful to bring out specific comparisons to facilitate discussion. For example, you can contrast item 16 (killing for food) with item 17 (killing for sport). Or, you can contrast item 3 (killing as a part of one's job) with item 7 (an act not related to one's job). There are many such pairings that can be discussed.

It won't be too long into the discussion before students begin to ask you to provide them with the "real definition" of aggression. Of course, one of the major points of the demonstration is that there isn't one. You can illustrate this by having students check the glossaries of several introductory texts. If you don't have any available, I've categorized a few from books that happen to be on my shelf:

- Definitions that require action, intent, and a human target:
  - "Behavior aimed at doing harm to others…." (Morris & Maisto)
  - "Any action carried out with the intent of harming another person" (Coon)
  - "Any behavior that is intended to hurt someone, either physically or verbally" (Weiten)
- Definitions that don't require a human target:
  - "Any physical or verbal behavior intended to hurt or destroy" (Myers)
- Definitions that require harm and a human victim:
  - "Intentional injury or harm to another person" (Feldman)

Several authors (Nevid and Rathus are examples) don't define the concept.

I close the discussion by emphasizing the importance of defining concepts in psychology. Concepts like aggression may lead to substantial disagreement despite the assumption that "everyone knows what this means."

This activity is adapted from:

"Defining Aggression: An Exercise for Classroom Discussion" by Ludy T. Benjamin, Jr., which appeared in *Teaching of Psychology* (1985, February), *12*, pp. 40–42.

The aggression questionnaire was adapted by Ludy Benjamin from:

Johnson, R. N. (1972) *Aggression in man and animals*. Philadelphia: Saunders.

Krech, D., Crutchfield, R. S., Livson, N., Wilson, W. A., & Parducci, A. (1982). *Elements of psychology* (4th ed.). New York: Knopf.

What is aggression? Check the items you think represent aggression.

_____ 1. A spider eats a fly.

_____ 2. A soldier shoots an enemy at the front line.

_____ 3. The warden of a prison executes a convicted criminal.

_____ 4. Two wolves fight for the leadership of the pack.

_____ 5. A juvenile gang attacks members of another gang.

_____ 6. Two men fight for a piece of bread.

_____ 7. A man viciously attacks a cat.

_____ 8. A man, while cleaning a window, knocks over a flowerpot that, in falling, injures a pedestrian.

_____ 9. A girl kicks a wastebasket.

_____ 10. Mr. X, a notorious gossip, speaks ill of many people he knows.

_____ 11. A man mentally rehearses a murder he is about to commit.

_____ 12. An angry son purposely fails to write to his mother, who is expecting a letter and will be hurt if none arrives.

_____ 13. An enraged boy tries with all his might to inflict injury on a larger bully but is not successful in doing so. His efforts simply amuse the bigger boy.

_____ 14. A man daydreams of harming his enemy but has no hope of doing so.

_____ 15. A senator does not oppose the escalation of bombing to which he is morally opposed.

_____ 16. A farmer beheads a chicken and prepares it for dinner.

_____ 17. A hunter kills an animal and mounts it as a trophy.

_____ 18. A dog snarls at a mail carrier but does not bite.

_____ 19. A physician gives a flu shot to a screaming child.

_____ 20. A boxer gives his opponent a bloody nose.

_____ 21. A Girl Scout tries to assist an elderly woman but trips her by accident.

_____ 22. A police officer shoots a bank robber who is trying to escape.

_____ 23. A tennis player smashes her racket after missing a volley.

_____ 24. A person commits suicide.

_____ 25. A cat kills a mouse, parades around with it, and then discards it.

Activity 55: Psychological Perspectives

Contributed by J. Kevin Denson
Kempsville High School
Virginia Beach, Virginia

Mr. Denson has been the psychology teacher at Kempsville High School for 20 years. He has been teaching AP Psychology for 13 years. He is also the social studies department chair.

Several times during the year, I ask my students to dissect a current event using psychological perspectives of behavior. This activity provides a nice blend of helping the students remember the perspectives of behavior and connecting the current events of human behavior together. I find this activity helpful because we usually discuss the perspectives very early in the school year, and so when I make reference to the perspectives later, the students are sometimes lost.

Some of the previous current events I have used successfully are:

- School shootings (see example on next page)
- Terrorist attacks
- Road rage
- Adulterous behavior
- Barry Bonds scandal
- Bill Clinton/Monica Lewinsky
- NBA brawl in Detroit
- Mark Foley
- Genocide
- Andrea Yates

Psychological Perspectives

Current Event: School Shootings at Virginia Tech

On April 16, 2007, Seung-Hui Cho murdered 32 people and wounded many others before taking his own life. Try to explain Cho's behavior from the following perspectives:

Behavioral

Behavior genetics

Cognitive

Evolutionary

Neuroscience

Psychodynamic

Social-Cultural

From what you have read about this situation, which perspective did others use to explain his behavior?

Activity 56: Psychology PowerPoint Presentation

Contributed by Christine Farina
Kapaa High School
Kapaa, Hawaii

Ms. Farina was born in Los Angeles, California, and moved to Kauai, Hawaii, in 1970. Her love of dance, coupled with her love of teaching, inspired her to open a dance studio in Hanalei, where she taught ballet, jazz, and aerobics. In 1992, she retired from teaching dance and went back to private tutoring and teaching in a private intermediate/high school on Kauai. In 2005, she returned to public school teaching at Kapaa High, where she now teaches World History, Psychology, and Economics. Ms. Farina has one daughter and three grandchildren, all living on the beautiful "Garden Island" of Kauai.

I ask my students to make a PowerPoint presentation on a psychology subject.

Psychology PowerPoint Presentation

Assignment Guidelines:

This project is intended to provide you, the student, with an opportunity to learn about a particular topic and then present your findings to your class. The reports will be presented orally, and you will accompany your report with a PowerPoint presentation. Remember, your audience wants to be interested in your topic, so do your best to give a presentation that you, yourself, would enjoy seeing and hearing.

Please choose one of the following subjects to present:

1. Alzheimer's disease
2. Anxiety disorder
3. Phobias (discuss phobias in general and pick one phobia to discuss in depth)
4. Self-esteem
5. Peer pressure
6. Autism
7. Bipolar disorder
8. Effects of television/media on violence
9. Obsessive-compulsive disorder (OCD)
10. Dyslexia
11. Eating disorders (bulimia [purging], anorexia)
12. Steroid use
13. Memory improvement techniques
14. Post-traumatic stress disorder (PTSD)
15. Computer and/or Internet addiction
16. Panic attacks and panic disorder
17. A particular psychology career
18. Schizophrenia

---

19. Teen suicide

20. Tourette's syndrome

21. Freud and the "Ego"

22. Comparison of the social development of girls and boys

23. Methamphetamines: effects on the brain and treatment

24. Effects of cigarettes and nicotine on the body and brain

25. Hallucinogens: effects and treatment

26. Alcohol addiction

27. Down syndrome

28. Use of forensic psychology

29. Sudden infant death syndrome (SIDS)

30. Other? List your suggestion here

To help you keep on track, I have set a timeline for various stages of this project:

1. First deadline—Turn in an outline of the main points and information to be presented.

2. Second deadline—Turn in a rough draft or note cards of the information to be presented. Keep in mind, I am not collecting written final reports (unless you feel that would be helpful to you), but I do want to see a rough draft of the information you plan to cover in this presentation. Also, I *do* want to see a bibliography with three sources (minimum one book) to be turned in when you give your oral report.

3. Third deadline—Turn in a layout plan for your PowerPoint presentation. PowerPoint slides shall consist of (1) a title slide with the topic name, your name, date, and a background picture; (2) picture slides when/if appropriate and bullet point information (*do not* cut/paste chunks of information); and (3) a wrap-up slide that has the main points your audience should know about your topic. The bibliography will be turned in with the oral presentation.

4. Fourth deadline—The presentations will begin in class. Everyone should be prepared by this date. The order of presentations will be randomly selected. Not being prepared on the day you are to present will result in loss of points. The presentation time should be approximately five to 10 minutes in length.

Scoring:

10 points—Turning in the completed outline on time

10 points—Turning in the rough draft and bibliography on time

40 points—Quality of information given in the report (thoroughness, organization, effective introduction and conclusion, overall knowledge of the topic)

40 points—Quality of the oral presentation (speaking voice [volume, speed], eye contact [*do not* read notes], posture [standing up straight, not fidgeting], PowerPoint slides [meet set requirements, effectiveness, thoroughness, relevance, lack of errors])

This project will constitute 20% of your grade this quarter.

We will be using the library and/or computer lab once or twice a week, but please understand that this assignment also constitutes your homework for this class. Remember: make a plan/schedule and stick to it! Flash drives are extremely useful for transferring work to and from school. I would advise you to get one, especially if you have access to PowerPoint at home.

Activity 57: Applying Psychology to Your Life

Contributed by Beth Ferns
Hudson High School
Hudson, Massachusetts

Ms. Ferns has been a teacher for 16 years, with six years at the middle school level and 10 years at the high school level. She presently teaches AP Psychology, General Psychology, Honors and regular Contemporary Legal Issues, and Honors Criminology as part of the online Virtual High School. She is a National Board–certified teacher in high school social studies. She is also an adjunct faculty at Lesley University in Cambridge, Massachusetts, in the graduate education department and at Southern New Hampshire University where she teaches in the education and sociology departments. Ms. Ferns has both a bachelor of science degree and a master of science degree in criminal justice with a specialization in forensic criminology. She also has a master's degree in education. In her spare time, Ms. Ferns enjoys spending time on her family's boat with her husband, three children, two stepchildren, and her mother. She loves to read and, when time permits, to catch episodes of *Law & Order* and *CSI*. She follows the Red Sox and Patriots faithfully. Ms. Ferns would also like to acknowledge the collaboration of her former student intern, Alexandra Agrillo, in the development of this lesson.

This project can be used with both AP and General Psychology classes. For this assignment, students are asked to demonstrate knowledge of course concepts by applying them directly to their own lives. Students may demonstrate mastery in a variety of methods. Students have made PowerPoint presentations, timelines, scrapbooks, board games, poems, stories, video interviews, and even a dialogue between a therapist and a patient.

Applying Psychology to Your Life

The purpose of this project is for students to demonstrate their understanding of the course by connecting content topics to their own lives. This can be accomplished through a variety of methods, such as those outlined below. The list below contains suggestions; alternate methods of presentation can be discussed.

Requirements:

1. Students must choose 10 of the 12 subject areas listed below and demonstrate a connection between those subjects and their own lives. The example topics for each subject are suggestions; you are not limited to using only these examples. Any examples you generate must have a clear connection to the chapters.
2. The connections must clearly demonstrate your understanding of the topics.
3. Connections may be made in a variety of ways, such as those listed below. Or you may suggest an alternative form of presentation.
4. Subjects (choose one example per subject):
   a. Research Methods
      – example of a time in your life when you have participated in or directed a form of research
   b. Biological Bases of Behavior
      – examples of behavior influenced by hormones
      – examples from hemispheric specialization
      – examples from genetics (a trait shared with a parent, etc.)
   c. Sensation and Perception
      – examples from experiences with your senses (getting glasses, hearing something incorrectly that caused a problem)
      – example where your perceptions were not true
   d. States of Consciousness
      – examples from dreams or daydreams
      – examples from your sleep patterns
      – examples from experiences with people who have abused drugs or alcohol
   e. Learning
      – example of some type of operant conditioning
      – example of cognitive learning
      – example of vicarious learning
   f. Memory
      – example of a vividly recalled memory or failed memory
   g. Cognition/Language
      – example from your language development
      – example of strategies used to solve a problem
   h. Life Span
      – specific landmark development in childhood or adolescence
   i. Motivation/Emotion
      – example of something by which you are extremely motivated
      – example connecting you to theories of emotion

(continued)

     j. Personality

         – example connecting your life to what a theorist would say about you

     k. Abnormal Behavior

         – example from your life when you have had to deal with someone with abnormal behavior

         – example of defense mechanisms you may have used

     l. Social Psychology

         – examples of how you form an opinion

         – examples of discrimination or prejudice you've experienced

         – example of a particular social influence that impacts your behavior

Topic Ideas:

Video timeline, written timeline, cartoon, poem, short story, monologue, song, visual art with captions, retrospective biography, interview, video biography, rap, PowerPoint presentation, play, or any other appropriate idea

(continued)

Category	5 Advanced	4 Proficient	3 Sufficient	2 Minimal	1 Needs Improvement
Content (this portion is weighted double)	−Contains numerous pertinent details −Makes excellent application of course content −Course content is evident in project −Exceeds required number of topics −Content presented in an extremely creative manner	−Contains good details −Makes good application of course content −Meets required number of topics −Course content is evident in project −Format of content shows creativity	−Contains adequate details −Makes some connections to course content −Meets required number of topics −Course content is present but not clearly evident in project −Format of content shows some creativity	−Contains limited details −Makes few connections to course content −Has six to nine required topics −Course content is difficult to discern −Format of presentation shows limited creativity	−Has few or no details −Makes few or no connections to course content −Has fewer than six required topics −Course content lacking or extremely difficult to discern −Format of presentation lacks creativity
Organization	−Opening clearly identifies topic −Ideas organized to maximize understanding of topic −Contains an excellent summary of ideas	−Opening includes good introduction to topic −Ideas are well organized −Includes a good summary of ideas	−Includes an opening statement −Ideas flow in an orderly manner −Ideas are summarized at the end	−Opening does not clearly identify topic −Ideas are unorganized, do not flow smoothly −Incomplete summary of ideas	−Opening is confusing or doesn't clearly identify topic −Ideas lack organization, do not connect well −Summary of ideas is lacking
Delivery	−Presenters consistently speak loudly and clearly −Presenters make eye contact with whole audience −Excellent body posture and gestures −Visual aids show exceptional neatness and clarity −Speaks knowledgeably about topic, uses note cards as an aid but does not read from them	−Presenters usually speak in clear, loud voices −Good eye contact with most of audience −Good body posture and gestures −Visual aids show neatness and clarity −Speaks well about topic but reads from note cards several times	−Presenters inconsistently speak in clear, loud voices −Adequate eye contact with most of audience −Satisfactory body posture and gestures −Adequate visual aids −Relies heavily on note cards; reads frequently from note cards	−Presenters often inaudible or not clearly understood −Minimal eye contact with audience −Distracting movements or stiff posture and gestures −Reads consistently from note cards	−Presenters are inaudible or not clearly understood −No eye contact with audience −Distracting movements or rigid stance −Lacks note cards or reads directly from cards

Name _____

Points/20 _____

Activity 58: Cartoon Journal

Contributed by Barbara Pester
Lincoln North Star High School
Lincoln, Nebraska

Ms. Pester has been a teacher of psychology at North Star High School in Lincoln, Nebraska, for three years. In addition, she is an adjunct faculty member in the Human Services Division at Southeast Community College. She is also a member of Teachers of Psychology in Secondary Schools, an AP reader for the Educational Testing Service, and a member of the National Council for the Social Studies.

Students will assemble a portfolio of cartoons that illustrate various psychological concepts. A minimum of five cartoons will be collected and must be accompanied by a one- to two-paragraph description that clearly identifies how the cartoon illustrates the identified concept.

Cartoon Journal

Objectives:

Students will analyze cartoons using psychological theories, concepts, and themes.

Process:

1. You will be collecting cartoons from newspapers, magazines, or the Internet.
2. The cartoons will be glued to sheets of paper and then placed in a folder, binder, or notebook.
3. The source and the date should be identified below each entry.
4. Place a one-paragraph discussion of the specific psychological concept the cartoon illustrates directly beneath the cartoon.
5. Each journal will have five cartoons.

Points = 50